EUROPE IN YOUR POCKET

EUROPE IN YOUR POCKET

A STEP-BY-STEP GUIDE
AND TRAVEL ITINERARY

**BY RICK STEVES
EDITED BY GENE OPENSHAW**

Northcote House

British Library Cataloguing in Publication Data

Steves, Rick, *1955*–
  Europe in your pocket: a step-by-step
  guide and travel itinerary.— UK ed. —
  (Pocket travellers).
  1. Europe – Visitors' guides
  I. Title II. Openshaw, Gene III. Steves,
  Rick, *1955*– Europe in 22 days IV. Series
  914'.04558

  ISBN 1-85373-075-0

© 1988 by Rick Steves
UK edition © 1989 by Northcote House Publishers

Maps David C Hoerlein

All rights reserved. No part of this work may be reproduced, other than for the purposes of review, without the express permission of the Publishers given in writing.

This edition first published in 1989 by Northcote House Publishers Ltd, Harper & Row House, Estover Road, Plymouth PL6 7PZ, United Kingdom. Tel: Plymouth (0752) 705251. Telex: 45635. Fax: (0752) 777603.

Printed in Great Britain by BPCC Wheatons Ltd, Exeter

CONTENTS

How To Use This Book		7
Back Door Travel Philosophy		14
Itinerary		16
Helpful Hints		20
Tour 1	Arrive in Amsterdam	21
Tour 2	Amsterdam	26
Tour 3	From Holland to the Rhine	31
Tour 4	The Rhine to Rothenburg	37
Tour 5	Rothenburg ob der Tauber	41
Tour 6	Romantic Road to Tyrol	44
Tour 7	Bavaria and Castle Day	49
Tour 8	Drive Over the Alps to Venice	53
Tour 9	Venice	62
Tour 10	Venice–Florence	66
Tour 11	Florence–Italian Hill Towns	73
Tours 12, 13 & 14	Rome	77
Tour 15	North to Pisa and the Italian Riviera	89
Tour 16	Holiday From Your Holiday: The Italian Riviera	93
Tour 17	From the Italian Riviera to the Alps	94
Tour 18	Alpine Walking Day	98
Tour 19	Free Time in the Alps, Evening Drive into France	100
Tour 20	Colmar, Alsatian Villages, Wine Tasting	107
Tour 21	The Long Drive to Paris, Stopping at Reims	110
Tour 22	Paris	112
European Festivals		124
Europe by Train		126
Youth Hostels		127

Europe in Your Pocket

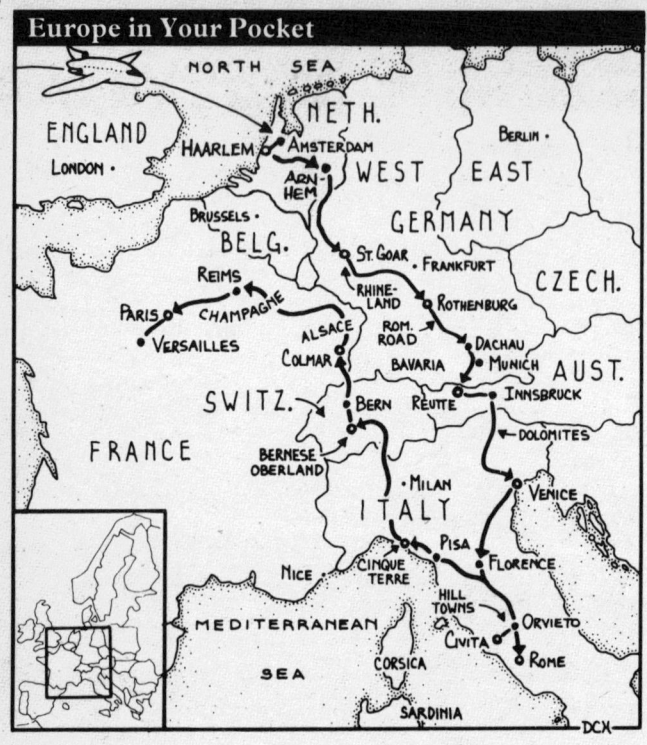

HOW TO USE THIS BOOK

This book is the tour guide in your pocket. It lets you be the boss by giving you the best basic European itinerary and a suggested way to use each section of that itinerary most efficiently. It's for do-it-yourselfers—with or without a tour.

Realistically, most travellers are interested in the predictable biggies—Rhine castles, Sistine Chapel, Eiffel Tower and beerhalls. This tour covers those while mixing in a good dose of 'back-door intimacy'—forgotten Italian hill towns, idyllic Riviera harbours and traffic-free Swiss Alp villages.

While the trip is designed as a car tour (3,000 miles), it also makes a marvellous three-week train trip. Each tour is adapted for train travel with explanations, options and appropriate train schedules.

Europe in Your Pocket originated (and is still used) as the handbook for those who join me on my 'Back Door Europe' tours. Since most large organised tours work to keep their masses ignorant while visiting many of the same places we'll cover, this book can serve as a self-defence manual for anyone taking a typical big bus tour who wants to maintain their independence and flexibility.

Three weeks' car hire (split two ways) or a three-week first-class Eurailpass costs £210 ($370) at the time of writing. For room and board, allow £20 ($35) a day for say 22 days, totalling £440 ($770). This is a feasible budget if you know the tricks. (If you don't know the tricks, see my book *Europe Through the Back Door*.) Add £100 or £200 ($200 or $300) fun money, and you've got a great European adventure for about £800 ($1400) plus the cost of getting to Amsterdam.

Of course, dot-to-dot travel isn't perfect, just as colour-by-numbers isn't good art. But this book is your friendly Frenchman, your German in a jam, your handbook. It's your well-thought-out and tested itinerary. I've done it—and refined it—20 times on my own and with groups. Use it, take advantage of it, but don't let it rule you.

Read this book from cover to cover, then use it as a rack to hang more ideas on as your trip evolves. As you study and travel and plan and talk to people, you'll fill it with notes. It's your tool. The book is completely modular and adaptable to any European trip. You'll find 22 tours, each with the same sections:

1. **Introductory overview** for the tour.
2. **Suggested Schedule** for the tour.
3. **Transport** plan for drivers, plus an adapted plan with schedules

for rail travellers.
4. List of **Sightseeing Highlights** (rated: ●●●Don't miss; ●●Try hard to see; ●Worthwhile if you can make it).
5. **Helpful Hints** on orientation, shopping, transport, day-to-day chores, timing.
6. An easy-to-read **map** showing all recommended places.
7. **Food and Lodging**: how and where to find the best budget places, including addresses, phone numbers, and my favourites.
8. **Itinerary Options** for those with more or less time, or with particular interests. This itinerary is flexible!

For each country there's also a **culture review**, and the back of the book includes a calender of local festivals.

Efficient Travellers Think Ahead
This itinerary assumes you are a well-organised traveller who organises your departure upon arrival, reads a day ahead in the book, keeps a list of all things that should be taken care of, and avoids problems whenever possible before they happen. If you expect to be systematic, you will. If you insist on being confused, your trip will be a mess. Please don't expect Europe to have stood entirely still since this book was written, and do what you can to phone ahead or double-check hours and times when you arrive.

When to Go
The best months to travel are May, June, September and October. Peak season (July and August) offers the best weather, the most exciting range of activities—and the worst crowds. During this very crowded time it's best to arrive early in the day and phone hotels in advance. (Phone from one hotel to the next; your receptionist can help you.)

Prices
I've priced things throughout this book in sterling and local currencies. These prices, as well as the hours, telephone numbers and so on, are accurate as of 1988. Things are always changing and I have tossed timidity out of the window knowing you'll understand that this book, like any guidebook, starts growing old even before it's printed.

Border Crossings
Crossing borders in Europe is generally easy—sometimes you won't even realise it's happened. If you do not hold a UK passport, you may need visas for some countries. Find what your own particular position is (your travel agent should be able to tell you) and

apply in good time. UK passport holders do not need visas for any of the countries in this itinerary.

When you do change countries you change money, postage stamps, and much more. Plan ahead for these changes (coins and stamps are of course worthless outside their home countries).

Language and Culture

You'll be dealing with a diversity of languages and customs; work to adapt. Europe's cultural stew is wonderfully complex. We just assume Germany is 'Germany'; but Germany is Tyskland to the Norwegians, Allemagne to the French, and Deutschland to the people who live there. While we think shower curtains are logical, many countries just cover the toilet paper and let the rest of the room shower with you. Europeans give their 'ones' an upswing and cross their 'sevens'. If you don't adapt, your 'seven' will be mistaken for a sloppy 'one' and you'll miss your train (and perhaps be cross with the French for 'refusing to speak English'). Fit in! If the beds are too short, the real problem is that *you* are too long.

By Car or Train

This itinerary works both ways. The book is written directly to the driver, with additional information for rail travellers. Each mode of transport has pros and cons. Cars are a headache in big cities, but give you more control for delving deep into the countryside. Groups of three or more go more cheaply by car. If you've got a lot of luggage go by car (you can even hire a trailer). Trains are best for city-to-city travel, and give you the convenience of doing long stretches overnight.

If you plan to hire a car, it's cheapest through your travel agent at home, by the week, with unlimited mileage. If your trip is longer than three weeks, your travel agent may find you a lease plan that will save you money. The petrol and tolls for this trip (if you take the motorways) will cost you about £275 ($500).

The Eurailpass gives you three weeks of unlimited first-class travel for £210 ($370), one month for £270 ($470). You must buy it from a travel agent outside Europe.

This pass is probably the rail traveller's best bet. Sample 1988 prices for second-class train tickets (first class is 50% more) are: Amsterdam–Frankfurt £31 ($54), Frankfurt–Munich £27 ($48), Munich–Venice £29 ($50), Venice–Rome £23 ($41), Rome–Interlaken £42 ($74). Interlaken–Paris £31 ($55), Paris–Amsterdam £29 ($50). In other words, individual second-class tickets for this trip would cost you the same as three weeks of unlimited first-class travel on a Eurailpass.

Scheduling

Your overall itinerary strategy is a pleasant challenge. Read through this book and note the problem days when most museums are closed. (Mondays are bad in Amsterdam, Munich, Dachau, Florence and Rome; Tuesday is bad in Paris.) Many museums and sights, especially large ones and those in Italy, stop admitting people 30 minutes before closing time.

Sundays have the same pros and cons as they do for travellers everywhere. Traffic in cities is light. Sightseeing attractions are generally open, but shops, banks, etc. are closed. Rowdy evenings are rare on Sundays. Saturdays in Europe are virtually week-days with earlier closing hours.

Things like banking, laundry stops, post office chores, and picnics should be anticipated and planned for. It's good to mix intense and relaxed periods. Every trip needs at least a few slack days. I've compiled the itinerary with every stop but three (Rhine, Italian Hill towns and Florence) for two nights in a row. This makes the speed of the tour much more manageable than a hectic series of one-night stands.

In order to function smoothly in Europe, you'll have to get comfortable with the 24-hour clock. I've used 'military time' throughout in this book. Everything is the same until 12:00. Times over 12:00 are pm. Just subtract 12 and you'll get the pm time (eg. 16:30 = 4:30 pm).

Speed

This itinerary can be done quite fast if all goes well . . . but all won't go well. A few slack days come in very handy, Eurail travellers should streamline things with overnight train journeys. I've listed many more sights than any mortal tourist would possibly want to see. They're rated so you can carefully make the difficult choices to shape your most comfortable, smooth and rewarding trip.

Keeping Up with the News (If You Must)

To keep in touch with world news while travelling in Europe, read the *International Herald Tribune*, which comes out almost daily via satellite from many places in Europe. British newspapers are frequently available. News in English will only be sold where there's enough demand—in big cities and tourist centres. If you are concerned about how some event might affect your safety contact the consulate or embassy in the nearest big city for advice.

Terrorism

Terrorism has no business affecting your travel plans. I spent ('survived') the summer of '86 in southern Europe. Viewed emotionally it seemed very dangerous. But statistically, regardless of what the terrorists are up to, the streets of Europe are no more dangerous than anywhere else, and safer than most. Just keep the risk in perspective and melt into Europe travelling like a temporary local. Terrorists don't bomb the hotels listed in this book—that's where they sleep.

Recommended Guidebooks

This small book is your itinerary handbook. Whilst you could have a good trip relying only on this book, I'd invest in a good directory-type guidebook listing recommended hotels, restaurants and cultural sights. I know it hurts to spend money on extra guidebooks, but when you consider the improvements they'll make to your holiday—not to mention the money they'll save you—not buying them would be perfectly 'penny-wise and pound-foolish'. Here is my recommended guidebook strategy.

General low-budget directory-type guidebook: *Let's Go: Europe* is ideal for student low-budget train travellers. Young, old, car or train, it's my choice for a supplementary directory-type guidebook. Arthur Frommer's individual country guidebooks (for Germany, France and Italy) cater to a moderate budget. Frommer's *Europe on $30 a Day* is very good, but helpful only for the big cities; for this trip, just rip out his chapters on Venice, Rome, Florence and Paris. If you like the *Let's Go* style, the individual books in that series (Italy and France) are the best anywhere.

Cultural and sightseeing guides: The tall green Michelin guides (Germany, Austria, Italy, Switzerland, Paris) have nothing about room and board but everything else you'll need to know about the sights, customs and culture. I find the new little blue American Express Guides to Venice, Florence, Rome and Paris even handier than the Michelin ones, but expensive.

Phrasebooks: Unless you speak German, Italian and French, you'd do well to invest in a phrasebook. Berlitz puts out great pocket guides to each of those languages, as well as a little book with 14 European languages covered more briefly (but adequately for me). Berlitz also has a pocket-sized 14-language menu phrasebook ideal for those galloping gluttons who plan to eat their way through Europe. Frommer's *Fast n' Easy Phrase Book*, covering Europe's four major languages (German, Italian, French and Spanish), is ideal for our itinerary.

Rick Steves' books: Finally, I've written this book assuming you've read or will read the latest editions of my books, *Europe Through the Back Door* and *Europe 101*, for a foundation of travel skills and art background to build upon. To keep this book pocket-sized, I have resisted the temptation to repeat the most applicable and important information already included in my other books; there is virtually no overlap.

Europe Through the Back Door gives you the basic skills that make this itinerary possible. Chapters cover minimising jet lag, packing light, driving or train travel, finding budget beds without reservations, changing money, theft and the tourist, tourism and terrorism, overcoming the language barrier, health, travel photography, laundry, itinerary strategies and more. The book also includes special articles on my 38 favourite 'Back Doors', seven of which are included in this tour (Hill towns, Cività di Bagnoregio, Cinqueterre, Romantic Road, Castle Day, Swiss Alps, and Alsace).

Europe 101 (co-written with Gene Openshaw) gives you the story of Europe's people, history and art. A little '101' background knowledge really helps Europe's sights come alive.

Mona Winks (co-written with Gene Openshaw) gives you a collection of self-guided tours through Europe's greatest—and most difficult—museums. *Mona Winks* covers many of the sights in this book, with one to three-hour tours of: Amsterdam's Rijksmuseum and Van Gogh Museum; Venice's St. Mark's, the Doge's Palace and Accademia Gallery; Florence's Uffizi Gallery, Bargello, Michelangelo's David and a Renaissance walk through the town centre; Rome's Colosseum, Forum, Pantheon, the Vatican Museum and St. Peter's basilica; and Paris's Louvre, the new and exciting Orsay Museum, the Pompidou Modern Art Museum, and a tour of Europe's greatest palace, Versailles.

For this trip, I would buy: (1) *Let's Go: Europe* (rip out appropriate chapters), (2) *Mona Winks* (take only applicable chapters), (3) *Frommer's Fast n' Easy Phrase Book*, and (4) *Michelin's Green Guide for Italy*. I'd read *Europe Through the Back Door* and *Europe 101* at home before departing. Of all the books mentioned, only the Michelin guides are readily available in Europe.

Raise Your Dreams to Their Upright and Locked Position . . .

My aim is free to you, not chain you. Please defend your spontaneity as you would your mother. Use this book to avoid time-and-money-wasting mistakes, to get more intimate with Europe by travelling as a temporary local person, and as a starting point from which to shape your best possible travel experience.

Anyone who has read this far has the intellect needed to do this tour on their own. Be confident, enjoy the hills as well as the valleys. Judging from all the positive feedback and happy postcards we get from travellers who used earlier editions of the book, it's safe to assume you're on your way to a great

European holiday—independent, inexpensive and with the finesse of an experienced traveller. Europe, here you come.

BACK DOOR TRAVEL PHILOSOPHY

AS TAUGHT IN EUROPE THROUGH THE BACK DOOR

TRAVEL IS INTENSIFIED LIVING—maximum thrills per minute and one of the last great sources of legal adventure. In many ways, the less you spend the more you get.

Traditionally, travel writers promote the tourist industry. I travel the way you will, make lots of mistakes and learn lots of lessons. I understand the fears and apprehensions that stand between travellers and their dreams. I know how these concerns can cause us to shackle our footloose and fancy-freeness to a rigid calendar of reservations. Travel is freedom. It's getting away from our briefcases and three-piece suits. It's a break—and we need it. Here are a few of my beliefs:

Affording travel is a matter of priorities. Many people who 'can't afford a trip' could sell their car and travel for two years.

You can travel anywhere in Europe for £20 ($35) a day plus transport costs. Money has little to do with enjoying your trip. In fact, in many ways, the less you spend the more you get—spending more money only builds a thicker wall between you and what you came to see.

Experiencing the real thing requires candid informality: going 'Through the Back Door'.

A tight budget forces you to travel 'close to the ground', meeting and communicating with the people, not relying on service with a purchased smile. Never sacrifice sleep, nutrition, safety or cleanliness in the name of budget. Simply enjoy the local-style alternatives to expensive hotels and restaurants.

We are often too 'things-oriented' to travel well. Travel like Gandhi—with simple clothes, open eyes and an uncluttered mind. It's a gift to be simple. If things aren't to your liking, don't change the things—change your liking.

Extroverts have more fun. If your trip is low on magic moments, kick yourself and start making things happen. Dignity and good travel don't mix. Let your hair down.

If you don't enjoy a place, it's often because you don't know enough about it. Seek out the truth. Recognise tourist traps.

A culture is legitimised by its existence. Give a people the benefit of your open mind. Think of things as different—not better or worse.

Of course, travel, like the world, is a series of hills and valleys. Be fanatically positive and militantly optimistic.

Travel is addictive. It can make you a happier person, as well as a citizen of the world. Our Earth is home to five billion equally important people. That's wonderfully humbling.

Globetrotting destroys ethnocentricity and encourages the understanding and appreciation of various cultures. Travel changes people. Many travellers toss aside their 'home-town blinkers', assimilating the best points of different cultures into their own character.

The world is a cultural garden. We're working on the ultimate salad. Won't you join us?

ITINERARY

TOUR 1 Arrive at Amsterdam's Schiphol Airport. Pick up your car or validate your Eurailpass. Stay in Haarlem, a cosy small town near Amsterdam. Everything's so Dutch!

TOUR 2 A busy day of sightseeing in Amsterdam. Visit Anne Frank's house, take the canal orientation tour, have a picnic lunch in the park, and tour the Van Gogh and Rijksmuseums. Return to your base for an Indonesian feast, 'Rice Table'. This evening it's just you and small-town Holland.

TOUR 3 Drive to Dutch open-air folk museum at Arnhem, best in Low Countries. Wander through the local folk life. Drive through the eye of Germany's industrial storm, popping out on the romantic Rhine river. Check into a *gasthaus* on the Rhine. Dinner below a floodlit castle.

TOUR 4 Crawl through Rheinfels, the mightiest Rhine castle. Cruise the most exciting chunk of the river, from St. Goar to Bacharach. Picnic in the park at Bacharach, with free time left to explore the old town. *Autobahn* to Germany's walled medieval wonder town, Rothenburg.

TOUR 5 After an early-morning walk around the old city wall, grab breakfast and catch an introductory walking tour. The rest of the day is free for sightseeing or shopping (this is the best shopping town in Germany). Your evening is best spent in a beer garden.

TOUR 6 Morning, explore the Romantic Road, Germany's medieval heartland. Tour the concentration camp at Dachau. After a late lunch in a Munich beerhall, take a quick walk through the centre of Munich before driving farther south into Austria. Dinner and evening in Tyrolian town of Reutte.

TOUR 7 'Castle Day' today. Beat the crowds to 'Mad King' Ludwig's magnificent Neuschwanstein Castle. Visit the best example of Bavarian baroque-rococo style church architecture, the Wies Church. Time to explore busy Oberammergau before returning to your Austrian base to climb to the ruined castles of Ehrenburg and have a ride on a thrilling alpine luge. Your evening is free to find some Tyrolian fun. There should be a lot of slap dancing and yodelling going on.

TOUR 8 Morning free in Innsbruck's historic centre with time to enjoy its great Tyrolian folk museum. After a scenic drive over the spectacular Austrian Alps and into Italy, stop for a tour of the impressively preserved Reifenstein castle. Then drive on to Venice. Orientate yourself with a cruise down the Grand Canal and check into your very central hotel. After a typical Venetian dinner enjoy gelato, cappuccino, and the magical atmosphere of St. Mark's at night.

TOUR 9 Morning tour of highlights of Venice: Doge's Palace, St. Mark's, the belltower. Rest of day free for browsing, shopping or art. This evening it's time for famous 'Back Door Stand-Up-Progressive-Venetian-Pub-Crawl-Dinner'.

TOUR 10 Leave very early for the three-hour drive to Florence, birthplace of the Renaissance. All day in Europe's art capital with time to enjoy Michelangelo's David, the Duomo and the Uffizi Gallery. Evening in Florence's colourful other-side-of-the-river.

TOUR 11 Morning free in Florence for more art, shopping, gelati. Grab a picnic before driving south to the tiny time-passed village of Città di Bagnoregio, near Orvieto. After getting settled in Angelino's hotel, spend the late afternoon and early evening immersed in the traffic-free village magic of Città. Curl your toes around its Etruscan roots. Dinner at the village's only restaurant, or have 'bunny' at Angelino's. Drop into Angelino's Cantina if you like vino and late-night fun.

TOUR 12 Morning free to tour Orvieto, spend more time exploring Città or just relax at Angelino's before taking the brutal plunge into Rome. Drive your chariot into the city of Julius, Peter and Benito; check in and enjoy a short siesta. Fill the late afternoon and the cool early evening with the Caesar shuffle—a historic walk from the Colosseum, through the ancient Forum and over the Capitol Hill.

TOUR 13 The morning is filled with fascinating sights in the core of old Rome—including the incomparable Pantheon, a Michelangelo statue and some glorious (and very deceptive) church architecture. After a self-service lunch and a necessary siesta the afternoon is free, but there's so much yet to see: Mussolini's futuristic suburb, E.U.R.; Rome's ancient seaport, Ostia; shopping; the Villa Borghese—you'll have no trouble filling it. For a colourful evening, catch a taxi to the wrong side of Rome's Tiber river, an area called Trastevere. This is Rome's seedy, seamy land of laundry, card games, graffiti and football in the streets.

After an atmospheric outdoor dinner, tonight's walk takes us past
Rome's top night spots: Piazza Navona (for Tartufo ice cream),
the floodlit Trevi Fountain, Spanish Steps, and the world's biggest
McDonalds.

TOUR 14 Learn something about eternity by spending the
morning touring the huge Vatican Museum. Of course, your
reward for surviving Rome is the artistic culmination of the
Renaissance, Michelangelo's Sistine Chapel. Then, after a lunch
and siesta break, tour St. Peter's, the greatest church on
earth—and possibly anywhere else. Scale Michelangelo's 100-yard-
tall dome. The later afternoon and early evening is for the
'Dolce Vita Stroll' down the Via del Corso with Rome's beautiful
people.

TOUR 15 Drive north to Cinque Terre. Lunch and time to
climb Pisa's tipsy tower. Then, up to La Spezia, where you'll leave
your car and take the train into the Italian Riviera. Vernazza is
your headquarters village for this holiday from your holiday. Find a
room in a pension, hotel or private home. Fresh seafood, local
wine and romance.

TOUR 16 All day free for walking, exploring villages, swimming,
relaxing on the beach: fun in the sun. You'll fall in love with
this sunny, traffic-free alternative to the French Riviera. Evening is
free—be careful, there's lots of romance on the breakwater!

TOUR 17 Leave very early. Hug the Mediterranean to Genoa,
then head north past Milan into Switzerland. After a stop in
Italian Switzerland, Ticino, you climb over Susten Pass and tumble
into the lap of the Swiss Alps, the Bernese Oberland. After a
stop in Interlaken, you'll take the cable car to the stop just this side
of heaven, Gimmelwald. This traffic-free alpine fairy-tale village
has only one chalet-hotel, the Mittaghorn, and that's where you'll
stay. Walter will have a hearty dinner waiting.

TOUR 18 Today is walking day. You'll spend the day memorably
above the clouds in the region of the Jungfrau and the Eiger.
Dinner with fondue at Walter's. Evening: rub your partner's feet
with coffee-schnapps and Swiss chocolate while the moon rises over
the Jungfrau.

TOUR 19 Free morning in the Alps. Optional lift up to the
10,000-foot Schilthorn for breakfast and walk down. Or sit in
a meadow and be Heidi. Or shop and explore one of the villages of
Lauterbrunnen Valley. Lunch at Walter's or a picnic before driving

out of Switzerland and into France. Evening in Colmar, Alsace, where you'll check into Bernard's Hôtel Le Rapp.

TOUR 20 All day to explore historic Colmar and the Wine Road (Route du Vin) of the Alsace region. Lovely villages, wine-tasting tours, and some powerful art. Evening is free in cobbled Colmar. Don't miss this opportunity to enjoy the Alsatian cuisine—some of France's best.

TOUR 21 Long drive to Paris with midday stop for a picnic in Reims. Tour Reims's magnificent cathedral for a lesson in Gothic architecture. This is Champagne country and you can also tour a Champagne cellar—free tasting, of course. After checking in in Paris, learn the metro system and orientate yourself. From an Eiffel Tower or skyscraper viewpoint, you'll have an exciting opportunity to preview this grand city studded with famous and floodlit buildings.

TOUR 22 This itinerary's finale is a very busy day with a look at the best of Paris. Morning tour of Latin Quarter, Notre-Dame, Ile de la Cité and the historic centre of Paris. After a self-service lunch and a tour of the highlights of the Louvre, the late afternoon is free for more sights, shopping, or to walk along the glamorous Champs-Elysées. Evening trip up to Montmartre for a grand city view, people-watching, crêpes, visit to Sacré-Coeur church and free time to enjoy the Bohemian artists' quarter.

Hopefully you'll be able to give Paris another day and spend a day touring Versailles, Europe's greatest palace.

Basic Options
You can return home on the day of your choice (which you decide when you buy your ticket). Which city you return from is up to you. To return to Amsterdam from Paris is a six-hour drive or a five-hour, £30 ($50) train journey.

If you have a few extra days, you can start and/or end this tour in London. After three nights and two days there, with possible day trips to Bath and/or Cambridge, catch the £30 ($50), eight-to-ten-hour trip to Belgium or Holland. Boats go daily overnight from England to Hoek van Holland (near Delft) or Oostende (near the great town of Bruges). From Paris you're an easy eight-hour trip to London.

To add Greece, rearrange this itinerary starting in London, then proceeding with Paris, Amsterdam, Germany, Switzerland and Italy before catching the boat from Brindisi, Italy to Patras, Greece (24-hour crossing, several each day, free with Eurail). See the

Greek ruins, enjoy a holiday from your holiday in the sunny Isles, and fly home from Athens.

You could also fly to Frankfurt. You could easily start your tour there, picking up a hire car or catching a train at Frankfurt airport (it has a station), going to Rothenburg (a great first-night-in-Europe place), and finishing with a pleasant day on the Rhine within two or three hours of the airport and your flight home. Don't sleep in Frankfurt; just go to its station and catch the easy shuttle train service from there to the airport.

To make the trip shorter, easier—and less exciting—skip Italy by going from Austria directly to Switzerland.

My other Pocket Travellers — *Great Britain In Your Pocket, Spain & Portugal In Your Pocket, Germany Austria & Switzerland In Your Pocket, Norway, Sweden & Denmark In Your Pocket,* and *France In Your Pocket* offer a tempting way to double (or triple!) your holiday options.

Helpful Hints

Phone before going to the airport or ferry port to confirm that your departure time is as scheduled. Expect delays. Bring something to do—a book, a journal, some handwork—to make any waits easy on yourself. Remember, no matter how long it takes, it is worth it! If you arrive safely on the day you hoped, it's been a smashing success.

To Minimise Jet Lag if Flying a Long Distance

■ Leave well rested. Pretend you're leaving a day earlier than you really are. Plan accordingly and enjoy a peaceful last day.
■ During the flight, minimise stress by eating lightly, avoiding alcohol, caffeine and sugar. Whenever I get a chance I say, 'Two orange juices, no ice please.' Take walks.
■ After boarding the plane, set your watch ahead to European time: start adjusting mentally before you land.
■ Sleep through the in-flight film—or at least close your eyes and pretend.
■ When you arrive, keep yourself awake until a reasonable local bedtime. A long evening city walk is helpful.
■ You'll probably wake up very early the next morning—but ready to go.

TOUR 1

ARRIVE IN AMSTERDAM

Amsterdam's Schiphol Airport, seven miles out of town (and below sea level), is efficient, English-speaking and 'user friendly'. Like nearly every European airport, it has a bank that keeps long hours and offers fair rates. (To save time and avoid the bank queue, change money in the baggage claim area while your luggage is still coming.) Schiphol Airport also has an information desk, baggage lockers, on-the-spot car hire agencies, an expensive room-finding service, and easy public transport. Airport taxis are expensive. Go by bus or train. The airport has a station of its own. (You can validate your Eurailpass and hit the rails immediately, or, if you need maximum time from your train pass, buy the short ticket today and start the pass later.) Schiphol flight info: tel. 511-0432.

If you're heading for central Amsterdam, catch a train (16 minutes, for £1.30 (f4.50), leaving every 15 minutes); for Haarlem, catch bus No. 174 or 176 from just behind the airport station. For Delft and points south, the train is best—but explore your options at the information desk. Public transport in Holland is great. Buses will take you where trains don't, and bicycles will take you where buses don't. Bus stations, railway stations and cycle-hire places are usually together.

The Netherlands

- 13,000 square miles.
- 14 million people (1,050 per square mile).
- The Netherlands, Europe's most densely populated country, is also one of its wealthiest and best organised. Efficiency is a local custom. The average income is higher than America's. Forty per cent of the labour force works with raw materials or in food processing, while only eight per cent are farmers. Seventy per cent of the land is cultivated, and you'll travel through vast fields of barley, wheat, sugar beet, potatoes and flowers.
- Holland is the largest of 12 provinces which make up the Netherlands. Belgium, the Netherlands, and Luxembourg have united economically to form Benelux. Today you'll find no borders between these 'Low Countries'—called that because they're low. Fifty per cent of the Netherlands is below sea level, on land that has been reclaimed from the sea. That's why locals say, 'God made the Earth but the Dutch made Holland'. Modern technology and plenty of Dutch energy are turning more and more of the sea into fertile farm land. In fact, a new 13th province Flevoland, near

Amsterdam—has just been dried out.

■ The Dutch are friendly and generally speak very good English. Dutch cities traditionally have been open-minded, loose and liberal (to attract sailors in the old days), but they are now paying the price of this easy going style. Amsterdam has become a bit seedy for many travellers' tastes; enjoy more sedate Dutch evenings by sleeping in a small town nearby and taking day trips into the big city.

■ Dutch Money: The Dutch guilder (f, or FL) is divided into 100 cents (c). There are about 3.5 guilders to the pound. The colourful Dutch money has Braille markings.

■ The best 'Dutch' food is Indonesian (Indonesia is a former colony). Find any 'Indish' restaurant and experience a *rijstafel* (rice table) which may have as many as 30 exciting dishes. Local taste treats are cheese, pancakes (*pannekoeken*), Dutch gin (*jenever*, pronounced like "your neighbour"), beer and 'syrup waffles'. Yogurt in Holland (and throughout Northern Europe) is delicious and can be drunk right out of its plastic container. Breakfasts are big by continental standards.

■ The country is so small, level and well-covered by trains and buses that transport is no problem. Amsterdam, Rotterdam and The Hague are connected by speedy trains that come and go every ten or 15 minutes. All you need to enjoy a driving holiday here is a car, petrol and a map.

■ The Netherlands is a cyclist's delight. The Dutch average four bikes per family, and have put a small cycle track beside every big road. You can hire bikes at most stations and drop them off at most other stations.

■ Shops and banks stay open from 9:00 to 17:00. The industrious Dutch know no siesta.

Small Tour Headquarters near Amsterdam

Charming, cosy, easily reached from the airport by bus, and just 20 minutes by train from the centre of Amsterdam (£1.50 (f5), trains go every ten minutes), Haarlem is a handy base giving you small-town overnight warmth with easy access to the hotspots of Amsterdam. Haarlem is the home of Frans Hals (his house is a museum with several of his greatest paintings), Corrie Ten Boom ('The Hiding Place' at 19 Bartelijorisstraat is open Mon.-Sat., 10:00-16:30), and Holland's greatest church pipe organ (in the Grote Kerk, several free concerts each week). Most of all, it's a bustling Dutch market covered with legions of shoppers cycling home with bouquets of flowers. Enjoy Saturday and Monday market days when the square bustles like a Bruegel painting with cheese, fish, flowers, and lots of people. You'll feel very comfortable here.

Tour 1   23

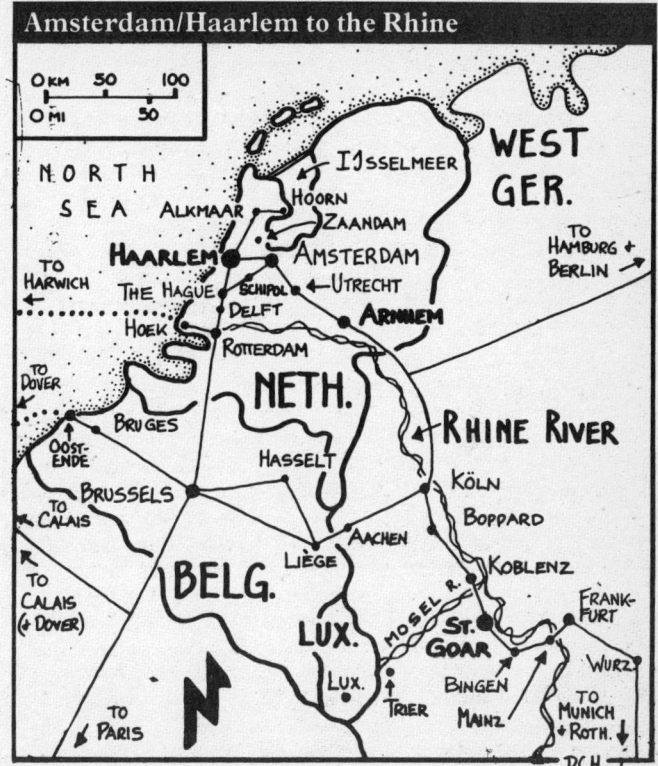

Eating and Sleeping

The helpful Haarlem tourist office (at the station, look for
VVV sign, open 9:00-18:00, tel. 023/319059) can answer all your
questions and find you a £10 (f35) room in a private home.
I stay at **Hotel Carillon** (Grote Market 27, Haarlem, tel.
023/310591) right on the town square. Frans, who runs the place,
speaks English and will hold a room with no deposit until
18:00 if you telephone him. He charges about £12 (f40) per person
in tiny loft singles or basic characteristic doubles (lace windows,
stee-e-ep stairs) with a fine breakfast. **Stads Cafe** (Zijlstraat 56-58,
tel. 023/325202) has bright and cheery doubles for £17-30
(f60-100). The **Youth Hostel (Jeugdherberg Jan Gijzen)** at Jan
Gijzenpad 3, tel. 023/373793, is about two miles from the
station (bus No. 2 or 6) and charges £5 (f18) with breakfast. Phone
first. Closed off season.

My favourite Dutch cuisine is Indonesian. Enjoy a *rijstafel*
feast at the friendly **Nanking Chinese-Indonesian Restaurant**,

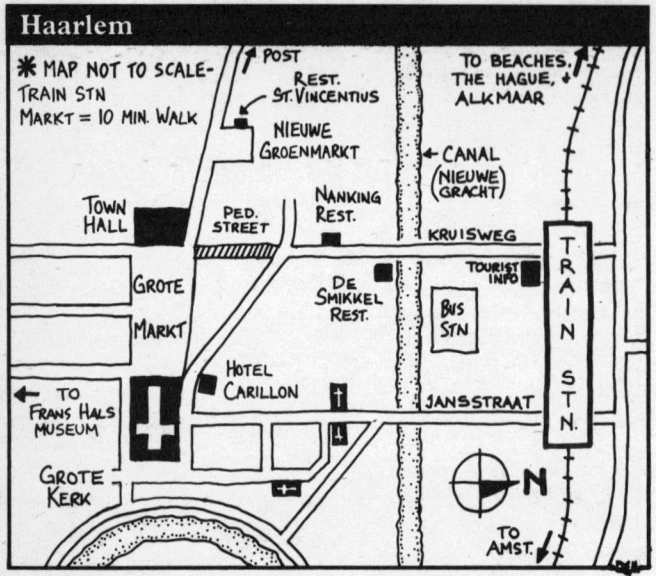

Kruisstraat 16, tel. 023/320706; a two-person £12 (f42) 'rice table' is plenty for three. Say 'hello' to gracious Ai Ping.

For a Dutch speciality, have a pancake dinner at the **Pannekoekhuis 'De Smikkel'** at Kruisweg 57. Hoek Parklaan speaks English and serves cheery dinner and dessert pancakes for £2.50 (f8) each. Closes at 20:00. For an interesting 'bread-line' experience with good basic/bland food and the cheapest price in town (£2 (f7)), eat at **St. Vincentius** (on Nieuwe Greenmarket, open Mon.-Fri. 12:00-13:30 and 17:00-19:00). The **Hotel Carillon** serves good food in a good atmosphere at moderate prices. For cheery tasty and bustling vegetarian meals (£4.50 (f16)) try the **Eko Eet Cafe**, Zijlstraat 39, near the Nieuwe Greenmarket. The **Stads Cafe** (Zijlstraat 56-58, tel. 023/325202, just off the square) offers great atmosphere, good food, and a reasonably priced meal of the day. Live music at weekends. For evening fun, the bars near the church between Jansstraat and Lange Begijnestraat are colourful and lively.

Remember, if you're returning to Haarlem before going home, reserve and pay for your last night's hotel room now. You can leave any unneeded luggage there (free) until you return. Taxis and buses can get you out to the airport easily.

Delft

Delft, peaceful as a Vermeer painting (he was born there) and lovely as the porcelain made there, is another safe, pleasant and very comfortable place to break into Holland and Europe. Delft is 60 minutes by train south of Amsterdam. Trains (£4 (f15)) depart every half hour. While Delft lacks major sights, it's a typically Dutch town with a special soul. You'll enjoy it best just wandering around, watching people, munching local 'syrup-waffles', or gazing from the canal bridges into the water and seeing the ripples play games with your face. The town bustles during its Saturday morning market. Its colourful Tuesday market attracts many traditional villagers. A town-wide sound system fills the colourful streets with pleasant music to browse by.

Reservations are unnecessary in Delft. Just drop in or phone from the airport. Delft has several simple hotels on its market square, the best being **Hotel Monopole**, (tel. 015/123059). Say 'hello' to Luke. £25 (f90) doubles include breakfast; Luke also serves 56 varieties of pancakes. Address: Markt, Delft. **Hotel Radhus** is also good. **Hotel Central** (Wijnhaven 6, 2611 CR, Delft, tel. 015/123442, located between the station and the square) is good but charges about £40 (f140) per double.

The **Peking** Chinese-Indonesian restaurant (two minutes off square, tel. 015/141100) serves a grand *rijstafel* Indonesian feast for about £7 (f25).

TOUR 2

AMSTERDAM

While Amsterdam has grown a bit seedy for many people, it's still worth a full day of sightseeing on even the busiest itinerary. The central station is your starting point (great tourist information, cycle hire, trains to all points). Damrak is the 'main street' axis connecting the station with the Dam Square (people-watching and hang-out centre) and the Royal Palace. The town's 90 islands, with hundreds of bridges and the series of concentric canals laid out in the 17th century offer an Old-World wonderland to explore. The city's major sights are within walking distance of the Dam Square. 'Amsterdam in a day' is, if not thorough, very exciting. Plan your time carefully, have a big breakfast and get up and go. You'll sleep well tonight.

Suggested Schedule

9:00	Anne Frank House, Westerkerk.
10:00	Palace, Dam Square, walk to Spui in Kalverstraat, Amsterdam's bustling pedestrian-only shopping street. Visit the Begijnhof.
12:00	Lunch, possible picnic.
13:00-17:00	Museums. Divide your time between Rijks, van Gogh and Stedelijk (modern art) museums, according to your interest.
17:00	Walk through Leidseplein (night-club centre) to Muntplein (flower market along canal) to Spui. Take the hour-long canal boat tour.
19:00	Walk past the Dam Square, through the red light district and sailors' quarters, possibly stopping for an Indonesian dinner on Bantammerstraat, and back to the central station, returning to your out-of-town base.

As you can—and will—see, Amsterdam and environs could easily fill a second day.

Sightseeing Highlights

●●●**Rijksmuseum**—Start your visit with a free, short slide show on Dutch art (every 20 minutes all day). Concentrate on the Dutch Masters: Rembrandt, Hals, Vermeer and Steen. Buy the cheap museum map and plan your attack. The book-shop has good posters, prints, slides and handy theme charts to the museum. There is also a cafeteria. (Tues.-Sat. 10:00-17:00, Sun. 13:00-17:00.)

● ● ●**Van Gogh Museum**—next to Rijksmuseum. This outstanding and user-friendly museum is a stroll through a beautifully displayed garden of Vincent's work. Don't miss it. (Tues.-Sat. 10:00-17:00, Sun. 13:00-17:00.) If you plan on collecting posters, buy a cardboard tube here.

Stedelijk Modern Art Museum—Next to Van Gogh, this place is fun, weird and refreshing (especially The Beanery by Kienholz). Open daily 11:00-17.00.

● ●**Anne Frank House**—A fascinating look at the hideaway where young Anne hid when the Nazis occupied the Netherlands. Pick up the English pamphlet at the door and don't miss the thought-provoking Neo-Nazi exhibit in the last room. Unfortunately, Fascism smoulders still. (Mon.-Sat. 9:00-17:00, Sun. 10:00-17:00.)

Royal Palace interior—July and August, 12:30-16:00.

Westerkerk—Next to Anne Frank's this landmark church, with Amsterdam's tallest steeple, is worth climbing for the view. (Be careful: on a hot day Amsterdam's rooftops sprout nude sun-worshippers.) Erratic hours.

● ●**Canal Boat Tour**—These long, low, tourist-laden boats leave constantly throughout the town for a good, but uninspiring, 60-minute multilingual £2 (f5) introduction to the city. No fishing, but bring your camera for this relaxing orientation.

Begijnhof—A tiny, idyllic courtyard in the city centre where the charm of old Amsterdam can still be felt. Visit the Hidden Church. On Begijnensteeg Lane, just off Kalverstraat between Nos. 130 and 132. The fine Amsterdam historical museum is just next door.

Rembrandt's House—Interesting for his fans. Lots of sketches. (Jodenbreestraat 4, 10:00-17:00, Sun. 13:00-17:00.)

Shopping—Amsterdam brings out the browser even in those who were not 'born to shop'. Shopping highlights include: Waterlooplein (flea market), various flower markets, (along Singel Canal near the mint tower or 'Munttoren'), diamond dealers (free tours), and Kalverstraat, the best walking/shopping street (parallel to Damrak).

Heineken Brewery Tours—For a first-hand look at this popular brewery—and plenty of tasting—join the long queue for the 9:00 or 11:00 tour.(Near the Rijksmuseum at Helstraat 30.)

Red Light District—Europe's most interesting ladies of the night shiver and shimmy between the station and the *Oudekerk* along Voorburgwal. It's dangerous at night, but a fascinating walk any time after noon.

● ●**Hire a Bike**—Roll through the city with ease (suggested cycle tour available at tourist information office). In one day I cycled: through red-light district, to Our Lord in the Attic (hidden church at O.Z. Voorburgwal 40), to Herrengracht Mansion (at Herrengracht 605, typical old rich household), to Albert Cuypstraat Market (colourful daily street market), to a diamond-polishing exhibit, through Vondelpark (Amsterdam's 'Hyde Park', good for people-watching and self-service cafeteria lunch), to Jordaan district, to Anne Frank's, to Westerkerk (climbed tower), to Royal Palace, and down Damrak back to the station. Whew! You can hire bikes for about £3 (f12) per day (with a hefty £60 (f200) deposit) at the central station (long hours, entrance to the left as you leave the station).

Vondel Park—Amsterdam's huge and lively city park giving the best look at today's Dutch youth. (Forty per cent of the city's population is under 40.)

Eating and Sleeping

Good hotels in Amsterdam are expensive (£30 (f100) per double). Budget travellers will want to take advantage of the many alternatives: informal private hostels, formal youth hostels, the popular 'boatels', or student hotels. The **VVV** (tourist office) across from the station will find you a room (£1.30 (f4.50) fee) but they don't list the cheaper places. Try to insist on the 'unclassified' budget alternatives at the VVV. You'll meet lots of hotel hustlers in front of the central station with very cheap rooms. If you're just looking for a simple bed, these are generally a good bet.

Youth hostels include **Vondelpark** (Amsterdam's top hostel, right on the park, at Zandpad 5, £5 (f18), tel. 831-744), **Stadsdoelen YH** (just past the Dam Square, at Kloveniersburgwal 97, £5 (f18), tel. 246-832), **Christian YH Eben Haezer** (near Anne Frank's, Bloemstr. 179, scruffy but friendly, £4 (f15)).

'**Boatels**': There are a number of cheap houseboats around the station. You'll find several just to the left at the Oosterdokskade near the post office. They charge around £10 (f35) per person with breakfast.

The area around Amsterdam's museum square (Museumplein) and the rolicking nightlife centre (Leidseplein) is colourful but comfortable, convenient and affordable. Here, a few hotels offer good value double rooms with showers and breakfast for around £30 (f100). Each is easy to reach from the central station (train No. 1, 2 or 5) and are within easy walking distance of the Rijksmuseum. **King Hotel** (Leidsekade 85, tel. 020/249603), **Quentin Hotel** (Leidsekade 89, tel. 020/262187), **Hotel Titus** (Leidsekade 74, tel. 020/265758), and **Hotel de Lantaerne** (Leidsegracht 111, tel. 020/232221).

Dutch food is fairly basic. Picnics, Eetcafes, cafeterias and automatic food shops are the budget eaters' best lunch ideas. Amsterdam's best budget Indonesian restaurants are on Bantammerstraat just beyond the red-light district. Try Ling Nam at No. 3 or Azie at No. 7. A giant *rijstafel* will cost around £6 (f20) per person.

Helpful Hints

In Amsterdam, every Monday is 'Black Monday': museums are closed and shops are only open in the afternoon. Throughout the Netherlands, the VVV sign means tourist information. At Amsterdam's tourist information office (tel. 266444) consider the Falk map (best city map), 'Amsterdam This Week' (periodical entertainment guide). 'Use It' (student and 'hip' guide) lists cheap beds, etc. The trams are great; 'strip cards' for ten journeys cost about £3 (f10), or you can buy an all-day pass for buses, trams and metro for about the same. Get your tickets on your first journey. If you get lost, nearly any tram will rattle you back to the central station. Drop by a bar for a *jenever* (Dutch gin)—the closest thing to an atomic bomb in a glass.

Side Trips

Many day tours into the country are available from Amsterdam. Buses go to quaint nearby villages from the station. The famous towns (Volendam, Marken Island, Edam, etc.) are very touristy but still fun. Alkmaar is Holland's cheese town—especially fun (and touristy) during its weekly market, Fridays from 10:00 to noon.

Zaandijk has the great Zaanse Schans, a 17th-century Dutch village turned open-air folk museum where you can see and learn about everything from cheese-making to wooden shoe carving. Take an inspiring climb to the top of a whirring windmill (get a group of people together and ask for a short tour); you can even buy a small jar of fresh windmill-ground mustard for your next picnic. Zaandijk, a traveller's easiest one-stop look at traditional Dutch culture, includes the Netherlands' best collection of windmills. This free park is open daily, April to October, 9:00-17:00, closed out of season. Ten miles north of Amsterdam, 15 minutes by train: take the Alkmaar-bound train to Station Koog-Zaandijk and walk—past a fragrant chocolate factory—for eight minutes. Skip Zaandijk if you'll be visiting the even better folk museum at Arnhem tomorrow.

The energetic can enjoy a bicycle tour of the countryside. A free ferry departs from behind the Amsterdam station across the canal. In five minutes Amsterdam will be gone and you'll be rolling though the *polderland*. Local entrepreneurs arrange great cheap cycle tours from Amsterdam.

TOUR 3

FROM HOLLAND TO THE RHINE

Today's objective is to explore Dutch culture, climbing a windmill and studying a thatch in a huge and creative open-air folk museum, and then to get to Germany's romantic Rhineland in the most direct way.

Suggested Schedule

8:00	Drive from Haarlem to Arnhem.
9:30	Tour Arnhem's open-air folk museum.
12:00	Pancake lunch.
14:00	Drive to St. Goar or Bacharach on the Rhine, possibly with an hour stop in Boppard.
19:00	Dinner at hotel and evening free in St. Goar or Bacharach.

Transport

By car from Haarlem, skirt Amsterdam to the south on the E9 following signs to Utrecht, then the E12 east to Arnhem. Take the Apeldoorn exit (after Oosterbeek exit, just before Arnhem). Signs will direct you to the nearby Openlucht Museum.

From Arnhem, cross into Germany and follow the *autobahn* through the eye of Germany's industrial storm, the tangled urban mess around Düsseldorf and Essen. Past Köln get on the E5, then cross the Rhine on *Autobahn* 48 towards Koblenz. Take the first Koblenz exit to cross the Mosel River into town (from the bridge, you can see the Mosel River on your right and the Deutches Ecke where the Rhine and Mosel merge on your left).

Past through boring Koblenz quickly, following signs to road No. 9 (to Boppard and Mainz) along the Rhine's west bank. As you leave Koblenz you'll see the huge brewery of Königsbacker and the yellow castle of Stoltzenfels.

Boppard is worth a stop. Park near the centre. Just above the market square are the remains of a Roman wall. In the square, buy the little Mainz-Koblenz Rhine-cruise guidebook (£2 (6DM)) with map. Below the square is a fascinating church. See carved Romanesque lunatics at the doorway. Inside, notice the 1,500-year-old Christian symbols, on the wall to the right of the entrance, and the typical painted arches. (Most old churches were painted this way.) On the arches near the river, note the high-water (*hoch Wasser*) marks from various flood years. St. Goar is just a few minutes upstream. Marksburg Castle (the only castle on the Rhine

not destroyed by the French), across the river from the village of
Spey, makes a great photo.

Trains make the 70-minute trip from Amsterdam to Arnhem
every hour. At Arnhem station just ask for the bus to the
Openlucht Museum. If you'd prefer a direct Amsterdam-Rhine
train, you can skip Arnhem, enjoy rural and village Holland for
half a day, then zip directly from Amsterdam to Koblenz in $4\frac{1}{2}$
hours, and on to St. Goar for dinner. Or you can leave Amsterdam
early and stop off in historic Köln. There are plenty of small milk-
run trains to take from Koblenz to St. Goar.

Sightseeing Highlight

● ● ● **Arnhem's Open Air Dutch Folk Museum**—An hour
east of Amsterdam in the sleek city of Arnhem is Holland's best
folk museum. You'll enjoy a huge park of windmills, old farms,
traditional crafts in action and a pleasant education-by-immersion
in Dutch culture. Buy the English guidebook for a fascinating
rundown on each historic building. Tel. 085/57611. Free guided
tours for groups with one week's notice.

The shops and craftspeople break from 12:00 to 13:00. Enjoy a
rustic lunch at the Pancake House (No. 74 on museum maps). The
Veluwa (meaning 'swamp') pancake is a meal in itself for £2.50 (f9).

Also near Arnhem is the Hoge Veluwe National Park— Holland's
largest—which is famous for its Kroller-Muller museum. This
huge and impressive modern art collection, including 276 paintings
by Vincent Van Gogh, is set deep in the natural Dutch wilderness.
The park has lots more to offer, including hundreds of white-
painted bikes you're free to use to make your explorations more
fun. Pick up more information at the Amsterdam or Arnhem
VVV.

Germany

■ 95,000 square miles.

■ 65 million people, about 650 per square mile, and declining
slowly).

■ *Ja, Deutschland*. Energetic, efficient, organised, and Europe's
economic muscle man. Eighty-five per cent of its people live
in cities. Ninety per cent of the workers get a one-month
paid holiday, and during the other 11 months they create a gross
national product of about one-third the U.S.A's. Germany
is the world's fifth biggest industrial power, ranking fourth in steel
output and nuclear power, third in car production. It also
shines culturally, beating all but two countries in production of
books, Nobel laureates, professors and strudel.

■ While northern Germany is Protestant and the populace assaults life aggressively, southern Germany is Catholic, more relaxed and leisurely. The Bavarian and southern German dialects are to High (northern) German what the dialect of Yorkshire is to the South East of England.

Germany

■ Germany's most interesting tourist route today—Rhine, Romantic Road, Bavaria—was yesterday's most important trade route, where Germany's most prosperous and important medieval cities were located. As a nation, Germany is just barely 100 years old. In 1850 there were 35 independent countries in what is now Germany. In medieval times there were over 300, each with its own weights, measures, coinage and king. Many were surrounded by what we might call iron curtains. This helps explain the many diverse customs found in such a compact land.

■ Practice your German energetically because nearly half of this holiday is in German-speaking countries (Germany, Austria, Switzerland).

■ Germans eat lunch from 12:00 to 14:00 and dinner between

18:00 and 20:00. Each region has its own gastronomic twist, so order local house specials in restaurants whenever possible. Fish, pork and venison are good. Great beer and white wines are everywhere. (In much of Germany beer is the best value. Try the small local brands.) 'Gummi Bears' are a local gumdrop sweet with a cult following (beware of imitations: you must see the word 'Gummi'), and Nutella is a chocolate-nut spread speciality that may change your life.

■ German Money: The Deutschmark (DM) is divided into 100 Pfennig (pf). A mark is worth about 32p. So 3 DM equals about £1. To get pounds, divide the prices you'll see by three. (e.g. 60 DM equals about £20).

■ Banks are generally open 8:00-12:30 and 13:30-16:00, other offices from 8:00-16:00. August is a holiday month for workers—but that doesn't really affect us tourists.

Eating and Sleeping

The Rhineland has plenty of budget rooms (*zimmers*) and *gasthauses* offering fine rooms for about £7 (20DM) per person, including breakfast. St. Goar, Bacharach and a few other towns have hostels where you'll get a bed for £3.50 (10DM). Spend the later evening in a Weinstube, soaking up the atmosphere and some of the local Rhine wine.

In St. Goar I stay one mile north of town in the friendly riverside **Hotel Landsknecht** (tel. 06741/1693). Klaus Nickenig and family offer doubles for £25 (75DM) and a rather nice Rhine terrace. In town, and easier for those without wheels, is **Hotel Montag** (Heerstrasse 128, just across the street from the world's largest free-hanging cuckoo clock, all new rooms, £27 (80DM) doubles, tel. 1629). Mannfred Montag and his family speak English and run a good shop (especially for steins) adjacent to the hotel. The best £8 (25DM) hotel beds in town are at **Gasthof Stadt St. Goar** (Pumpengasse 5, tel. 1646, near station). **Gasthof Weingut Muhlenschenke** (actually a small winery with tasting for £2 (6DM) is your best cosy out-of-town bed (Grundelbach 73, tel. 1698, £9 (27DM) per person). St. Goar's best *zimmers* are the homes of Frau Wolters (Schlossberg 24, tel. 1695, on the road to the castle, great view, cosy, £7 (20DM)), Frau Kurz (Ulmenhof 11, tel. 459, two minutes from the station, £8 (24DM)). The St. Goar **hostel** is a big white building under the castle, run very 'Germanly', and is good value with £3 (9DM) beds and good £2 (6DM) dinners, tel. 06741/388.

The town of Bacharach, near St. Goar, has Germany's best youth hostel, a castle on the hilltop with a royal Rhine view called **Jugendherberg Stahleck**; it is closed from 9:00 to 17:00;

members of all ages are welcome; £4 (12.50DM) per bed, places
normally available in July and August; tel. 06743-1266. Steep
ten-minute climb on trail from town church or drive up.

The following **Bacharach** *zimmers* are central, charge about
£7 (20DM) and their owners speak some English: Gertrud
Aman (Oberstrasse 13, tel. 1271), Annelie Dettmar (Oberstrasse 18,
tel. 2979), Kathe Jost (Blucherstrasse 33, tel. 171), and Christel
Ketzer (Blucherstrasse 51, tel. 1617). My choice for the best budget
combination of comfort, hotel privacy with *zimmer* warmth,
central location and medieval atmosphere, is the friendly **Hotel
Kranenturm** run by Kurt and Fatima Engel. It is actually part of
the medieval fortification, and the former towers are now
round rooms. Located near the railway tracks (ask Kurt to explain
his special windows to you) at Langstrasse 30, tel. 06743/1308.
Great cooking and a wonderful Kranenturm ice-cream special
£8 (25DM)/person. For atmospheric dining elsewhere in Bacharach,
try the **Altes Haus**, the oldest building in town.

Sightseeing Options and Nearby Side Trips

● ● **The Mosel River**, which joins the Rhine at Koblenz, is more
pleasant and less industrial than the Rhine. Lined with vineyards,
tempting villages and two exciting castles (Cochem and Burg Eltz),
it's a super place to spend an extra day if you have one. Cochem is
the best base for the Mosel region. Berg Eltz is my favourite
German castle—near Munden, open 9:00-17:30, April-October.

● ● **Bonn**—Bonn was chosen as West Germany's temporary
capital after World War II when German unity was still expected.
Its sleepy, peaceful character seemed like a good place to plant
Germany's first post-Hitler government. Today it is sleek, modern
and, by big-city standards, remarkably pleasant and easy-going. It's
worth a look—not only to see Beethoven's house and the
parliament buildings, but also to come up for a breath of the real
world before diving into the misty romantic Rhine and Bavaria.

The tourist information office, directly in front of the station, is
excellent (8:00-21:00, Sun. 9:30-12:30, tel. 0228/773466, free room-
finding service). The market square and Münsterplatz are a joy,
as is the local shopping and people-watching. **Hotel Eschweiler**
(Bonngasse 7, tel. 0228/635385) is very good.

● ● **Köln (Cologne)**—This big no-nonsense city—Germany's fourth largest—has a compact and fascinating centre. Since the Rhine
was the northern boundary of the Roman Empire, Köln, like most
of these towns, goes back 2,000 years. It was an important cultural
and religious centre throughout the Middle Ages; even after World
War II bombs destroyed 95 per cent of the city, it remains, after
a remarkable recovery, a cultural and commercial centre as well as a
fun and colourful city.

Its *Dom*, or cathedral, is far and away Germany's most exciting Gothic church. (50 yards from the station, tours Mon.-Fri. at 10:00, 11:00, 13:30, 14:30 and 15:30, Sat. at 10:00 and 11:00.) Next to the *Dom* is the outstanding Romisch-Germanisches Museum, a fine Roman museum (Tues.-Sun. 10:00-17:00, Wed. and Thurs. until 20:00). You can view its prize piece—a beautiful mosaic floor—free, from the front window. The displays are in German only. The Wallrof-Richartz Museum has a new home between the Roman museum and the river. If you like modern and pop art, don't miss it. (Tues.-Sun. 10:00-17:00, Tues. and Thurs. 10:00-20:00, tel. 0221/2212379). The tourist information office near the station, opposite the *Dom's* main entrance, is very helpful (tel. 0221/2213345, daily 8:00-22:30).

Charlemagne's Capital, Open Air Folklife Museum, and **Phantasialand**—If you have an extra day, a number of interesting sights are within easy striking distance of Bonn and Köln. Aachen is a very historic town—the capital of Europe in 800 A.D., when Charlemagne called it Aix-la-Chapelle. The remains of his rule include an impressive Byzantine/Ravenna-inspired church with his sarcophagus and throne. The city also has an almost sensational newspaper museum and great fountains, including a clever 'arrange-them-yourself' version.

If you'd like to learn more about regional folklore, visit the Rheinisches Freilichtmuseum, an open-air museum in a lovely natural setting near Kommern. Take the Euskirchen-Wisskirchen *autobahn* exit southwest of Bonn.

And if you'd like to fight the lowbrow local crowds at a tacky second-rate local Disneyland, visit Phantasialand. It's popular enough to have its very own *autobahn* exit south of Bruhl between Bonn and Köln. You may see Mickey Maus.

TOUR 4

THE RHINE TO ROTHENBURG

Spend today exploring the Rhine's mightiest castle, cruising down its most famous stretch, and driving on to Rothenburg, Germany's best-preserved medieval town.

Suggested Schedule

7:30	Breakfast.
8:15	Bank and browse in St. Goar.
9:00	Tour Rheinfels Castle, explore St. Goar.
11:55	Catch the Rhine steamer, cruise and picnic to Bacharach.
13:00	Drive to Rothenburg.
17:00	Find hotel and get settled in.
Evening	Free in Rothenburg.

The banks open at 8:00 in St. Goar. Change enough money to get you through Germany. The small supermarket on Main Street, across from the world's largest free-hanging cuckoo clock, is good for picnic ingredients. Friendly Mr. Montag in the shop under the Montag Hotel has stamps and fine steins.

Sightseeing Highlights

●●●**The Rheinfels Castle**—The Rhine's biggest and most important castle is a 15-minute walk up the hill. The castle sits on several miles of spooky tunnels (bring your torch). If there's a guided tour available, take it. The castle opens at 9:00. The handiest guide book for this region is the small, red Mainz-Koblenz book with foldout Rhine map (about £2 (6DM)).

●●●**The Rhine River Cruise**—While the Rhine flows hundreds of miles from Switzerland to Holland, the chunk from Mainz to Koblenz is by far the most interesting. This stretch studded with the crenelated cream of Germany's castles, is busy with boats, trains and cars. It's easy to explore. While many do the whole trip by boat, I'd tour the area by train or car and cruise just the most scenic hour, from St. Goar to Bacharach.

If you're driving, the boat trip can present a problem. You can (1) skip the boat, (2) take a round-trip tourist excursion boat trip from St. Goar, (3) let one person in your group drive to Bacharach, prepare the picnic and meet the boat, or (4) take the boat to Bacharach and return by train, spending your waiting time exploring that old half-timbered town. I'd probably take the first

Best of the Rhine

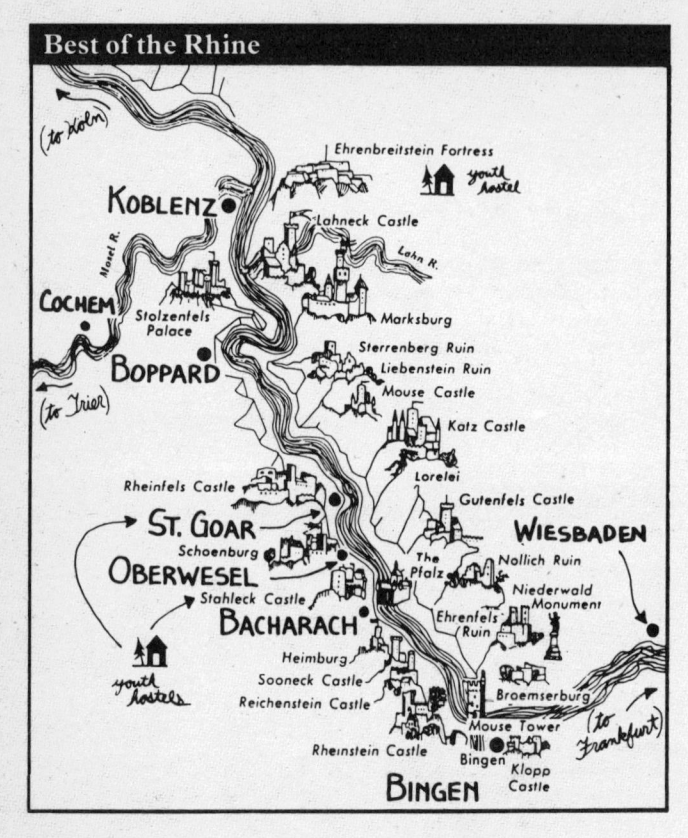

Map showing the Rhine region with locations including Koblenz, Cochem, Boppard, St. Goar, Oberwesel, Bacharach, Bingen, Wiesbaden; castles and landmarks: Ehrenbreitstein Fortress, Lahneck Castle, Stolzenfels Palace, Marksburg, Sterrenberg Ruin, Liebenstein Ruin, Mouse Castle, Katz Castle, Lorelei, Gutenfels Castle, Rheinfels Castle, Schoenburg, The Pfalz, Nollich Ruin, Stahleck Castle, Niederwald Monument, Ehrenfels Ruin, Heimburg, Sooneck Castle, Reichenstein Castle, Broemserburg, Rheinstein Castle, Mouse Tower, Klopp Castle; with youth hostels marked and arrows to Köln, Trier, and Frankfurt.

option and spend more time poking around with the car.

To catch the boat in St. Goar, be down at the Köln-Düsseldorfer dock at the far end of Main Street for the 10:15 boat (rush the castle, picnic in Bacharach) or the 11:55 boat (picnic on board). The one-hour trip to Bacharach costs about £3.50 (10DM) (free with Eurail) and tickets are easy to purchase at the dock five minutes before departure. The boat is never full. (Confirm times at your hotel.)

Sit on the top deck with your handy Rhine map-guide and enjoy the parade of castles, towns, boats and vineyards. If your boat is the *Goethe*, observe its grinding paddle-wheel engine. You'll pass, and hopefully survive, the seductive Lorelei—the huge rock from which, according to highly placed legendary sources, a beautiful maiden once lured medieval boats onto the rocks. (Any postcard rack will tell you her story in English.)

In Bacharach you'll find grocery shops, fresh cherries on sale

Tour 4

near the dock, and a great picnic spot in the riverfront park. Continue on, by car or train (about one per hour), down the Rhine to Mainz. From there, drivers enjoy the *autobahn* all the way to Rothenburg.

Transport
From Bacharach to Mainz there are plenty of good castles. After that you can hit the *autobahn*, skirting Frankfurt and setting *das auto-pilot* on Würzburg. You'll pass U.S. military bases, Europe's busiest airport, lots of lorries, World War II road vehicles and World War III sky vehicles. Just before Würzburg is the Rohrbrunn rest stop; stop here to let wonderful Herr Ohm at the tourist office help you; pick up his info on Bavaria, Würzburg, Rothenburg and the Romantic Road. He will even phone to confirm or help you find a room in Rothenburg (tel. 06094-220). Just before Würzburg take the *autobahn* exit marked

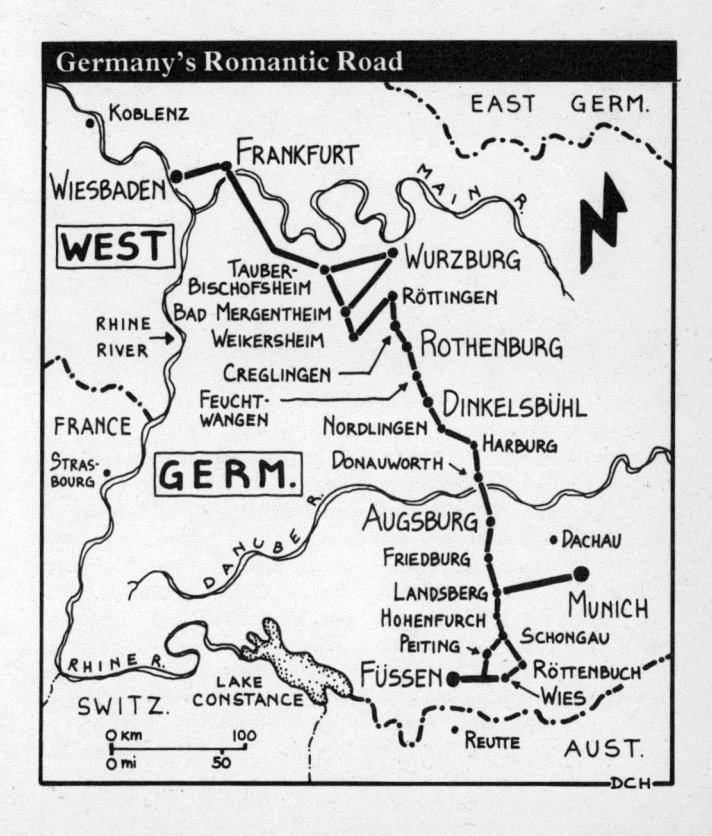

'Würzburgh/Stuttgart/Ulm, road No. 19'. Follow No. 19 south to just before Bad Mergenheim, where a particularly scenic slice of the Romantic Road will lead you right into Rothenburg. Or, if you're in a hurry and don't like romantic countryside, continue south on the new *autobahn*.

If you're travelling by train, your Eurailpass gets you onto the Rhine cruise and the Romantische Strasse (Romantic Road) bus tour free. The best hour-long cruise of the Rhine is from St. Goar to Bacharach. If you're really enjoying the cruise, stay on until Wiesbaden. If you get off at Bacharach, hourly trains link Bacharach with St. Goar and Frankfurt. Ask for schedule information at the boat dock.

The Romantic Road bus tour leaves Wiesbaden at 7:00 daily. A reservation is advisable only on summer weekends; just telephone 069-7903240 three days in advance. The best part of the trip is south of Rothenburg. You can take the train to Rothenburg, but it's tricky and takes about three hours: Frankfurt to Würzburg (many trains), Würzburg to Steinach (hourly), Steinach to Rothenburg (almost hourly). Get specifics at any German station. Enjoy an evening in that most romantic of medieval German towns, and catch the daily Romantic road bus on to Munich or Fussen at about 13:30.

While the Rhine is beautiful by boat, car and train, it also has a great riverside cycle track. Ask at stations for cycle hire information. This part of the Rhine has no bridges, but plenty of ferries.

Eating and Sleeping

Rothenburg is crowded with visitors but, since most are day-trippers, finding a room is no problem. From the main square (which has a tourist office with room-finding service), just walk down Schmiedgasse until it becomes Spitalgasse. This street has plenty of *gasthauses*, *zimmers* (£8 (25DM) per person with breakfast) and two good £1.50-a-night youth hostels (tel. 09861/4510 or 09861/7889). I stay at No. 28, **Hotel Goldenen Rose**, tel. 09861/4638, for about £8 (25DM) a night. Less expensive and very friendly is a room in the home of Herr Moser at Spitalgasse No. 12 (£15 (45DM) doubles, tel. 5971; speaks little English: talk slowly and clearly). Also good are **Gasthaus Raidel** (Wenggasse No. 3, tel. 3115; £8 (25DM) per person, will hold a room for a phone call), **Pension Poschel** (Wenggasse 22, tel. 3430, £7 (20DM), **Pension Becker** (Rosengasse 23, tel. 5562, £8 (25DM) and the friendly *zimmer* of English-speaking **Georg and Frida Ohr** (Untere Schmiedgasse No. 6 near the Medieval Crime Museum, tel. 4966, £13 (40DM) doubles).

TOUR 5

ROTHENBURG OB DER TAUBER

Rothenburg is well worth two nights and a whole day. In
the Middle Ages, when Frankfurt and Munich were just wide spots
in the road, Rothenburg was Germany's second largest city,
with a whopping population of 6,000. Today it's her best-preserved
medieval walled town, enjoying tremendous tourist popularity
without losing its charm.

Suggested Schedule

6:30	Walk around Rothenburg's medieval wall.
8:00	Back at your hotel for breakfast.
9:00	Visit Tourist Office to confirm your plans.
9:30	Shop, browse, climb city hall tower, see the Meistertrunk show.
12:00	Picnic in castle garden.
13:00	Free time or walk down to Detwang and Toppler's summer castle. Or take city walking tour.
16:00	Visit St. Jacob's Church to see carving.
17:00	Tour Medieval Crime and Punishment Museum.

Orientation

Pick up a map and information at the tourist information
office in the main square (9:00-12:00, 14:00-18:00, Sat. 9:00-12:00,
closed Sunday). Confirm sightseeing plans and ask about tours and
evening entertainment.

To orientate yourself, think of the town map as a head. Its nose
(the castle) sticks out to the left; the neck is the lower panhandle
part (with the youth hostels and my favourite hotel).

Too often Rothenburg brings out the shopper in visitors before
they've had a chance to appreciate the historic city. This is a
great place to do your German shopping, but first see the town.
The tourist information office has guided tours in English; also,
guided walks in English leave the Hotel Riemenschneider, most
days at 13:30, £1.30 (4DM). If none are scheduled, hire a private
guide; for about £15 (45DM), a local historian—who's usually
an intriguing character—will bring the ramparts alive. A thousand
years of history are packed between the cobbles. For a private
guide, call Karin Bierstedt (09861/2217) or Manfred Baumann
(4146).

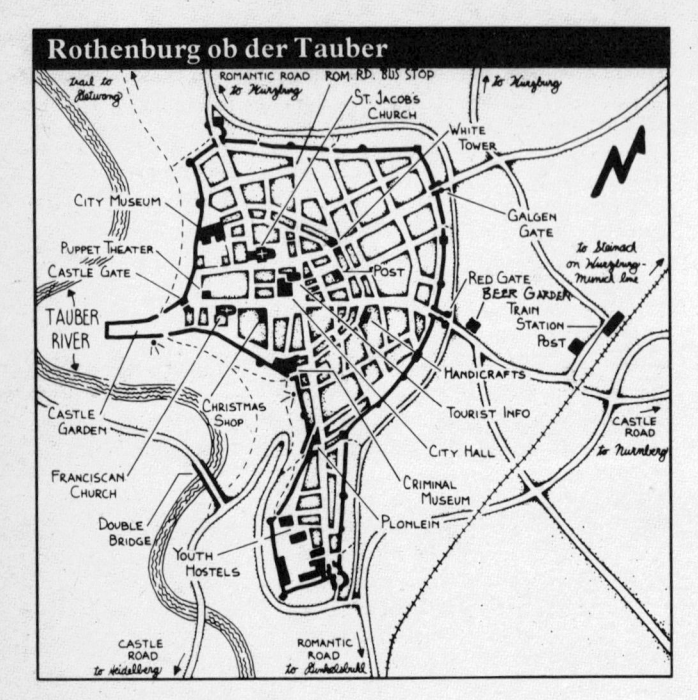

Sightseeing Highlights

●●**Walk the Wall**—Just over a mile around, Germany's best medieval wall offers great views, a good orientation and a good look at Rothenburg. It can be done speedily in one hour. Photographers will go through lots of film. The wall is best before breakfast or at sunset.

●●**Climb Town Hall Tower**—For a towering view of the town and surrounding countryside, take the rigorous but interesting climb up the city hall tower (9:30-12:30, 13:00-17:00, 1 DM).

●●**Medieval Crime and Punishment Museum**—This is the best of its kind, full of fascinating old legal bits and pieces, instruments of punishment and torture, even a special cage—complete with a metal gag—for nags. Exhibits in English. Open 9:30-18:00, £1.30 (4DM).

●●●**St. Jacob's Church**—Here you'll find the best Riemenschneider altarpiece, dated 1466, located up the stairs and behind the organ. Tilman Riemenschneider was the Michelangelo of German woodcarvers. This is the one 'must see' art treasure in town. Open daily 9:30-17:30, Sun. 10:30-17:30, 2DM.

Meistertrunk show in the main square at 11:00, 12:00, 13:00, 14:00, 15:00, 17:00 or 22:00. Join the ritual gathering of the tourists to see the re-enactment of the Meistertrunk story—the popular but fanciful tale of the mayor of the town who, in 1631, drank nearly a gallon of wine in one long gulp to placate an invading general and save the town from rape, pillage and plunder. You'll see his huge mug in the town museum.

● **Walk in the countryside**—Just below the Burggarten (castle garden), in the Tauber Valley, is the quaint, skinny 600-year-old castle/summer home of Mayor Toppler (open 10:00-12:00, 14:00-17:00). It's furnished intimately and is well worth a look. Notice the photo of bombed-out 1945 Rothenburg on the top floor.

Across from the castle, a radiantly happy lady will show you her 800-year-old water-powered flour mill called the Fuchsmühle. Down the road see the covered bridge and the many big trout. Complete your countryside stroll by walking to the little village of Detwang; it is actually older than Rothenburg and has another fine Riemenschneider altarpiece and a great local-style restaurant next to its campsite. The most direct path from Rothenburg to Detwang is from the Klingen Gate. The sunsets over the 'Tauber Riviera' and from the Burggarten Park will remind you what a great idea this holiday was. You can hire bicycles at the station (*bahnhof*), £1.70 (50DM) if you have a ticket or train pass, £3.40 (10DM) otherwise, open daily 5:00-18:30.

Shopping

Rothenburg is one of Germany's best shopping towns. Make a point to do your shopping here. (Post it home from the handy post office, which even sells boxes.) Lovely prints, carvings, wine glasses, Christmas tree ornaments and beer steins are very popular. The shop run by Anneliese Friese, just west of the tourist office on the corner across from the public toilet, is friendly, good and gives shoppers with this book a ten per cent discount. Anneliese will send purchases home for you (tax free) at her expense, change money with rates better than the banks, and give you a great free map of Rothenburg. Rothenburg has a good selection of Hummels.

For those who prefer to eat their souvenirs, the Backerei with their succulent pastries, pies and cakes are a tasty distraction. Skip the good-looking but bad-tasting Rothenburger Schnee Balls.

Evening Fun and Beer Drinking

The best beer garden for summer evenings is just outside the wall at the Rödertor (Red Gate). Closer to home, enjoy good wine, fun accordion music and a surly waiter at the **Plonlein Cafe** (Plonlein 4).

TOUR 6

ROMANTIC ROAD TO TYROL

This is a big and varied day. Get an early start to enjoy the quaint hills and rolling villages of this romantic region. (To make more time in Munich, I'd skip breakfast and leave by 7:00.) What was Germany's major medieval trade route long ago is today's top tourist trip. Drive through pretty Dinkelsbuhl and continue south, crossing the baby Danube River (Donau in German) to Dachau. Ponder the concentration camp and drive into Munich, the capital of Bavaria, for some beerhall fun and a quick look at Germany's most livable city. (Squeezing Munich into this tour rushes things—but I think it's worthwhile.) Then finish off the Romantic Road, driving on to Reutte in Tyrol, Austria—your base for tomorrow's 'castle day' and Bavarian explorations.

Suggested Schedule

7:00	Early departure, drive south on Romantic Road.
9:30	Tour Dachau, museum, film, grounds.
11:00	Drive into Munich for a beerhall lunch and a look at the town centre.
15:00	Drive to Reutte.
19:00	Dinner.
20:30	Tyrolian Folk Evening.

Transport

By car you'll be following the green 'Romantische Strasse' signs, winding scenically through the small towns until you hit the *autobahn* near Augsburg. Take the *autobahn* towards Munich (München), exiting at Dachau. Follow the signs marked 'KZ Gedenkstatte'. From Dachau, follow Dachauerstrasse into Munich. This is big-city driving at its worst, so check your insurance and fasten your seatbelt. You'll see the cobweb-style Olympic Village with its huge TV tower on the left. An easy option for drivers is to park there and take the underground (*U-bahn*) to Marienplatz (the city centre). Or, work your way right to the centre of things, setting your sights on the twin domes of the Frauenkirche—the symbol of Munich—and parking between that landmark church and the *bahnhof* (station). Your goal is to park as close to the centre as possible, explore it for a few hours, and head south following the *autobahn* signs to Innsbruck, then Fussen, Landsberg and Lindau. On weekdays leave by 16:00 to avoid the nightly traffic jam. (To skip Munich, from Dachau cross back over the *autobahn* following signs to Furstenfeld, then Inning, then Landsberg and on to Fussen.) Leave the Munich-Lindau *autobahn* at Landsberg and wind south again on the Romantic Road to Fussen. Just before Fussen you'll see hang gliders circling like colourful vultures and, in the distance, the white shimmering dream castle, Neuschwanstein. Follow the little road to the left to drive under it. If the weather's good, stop for a photo. Just over the Austrian border from here you'll find Reutte.

You may choose to take the *autobahn* south from Munich to Garmisch, a resort town at the base of the Zugspitze, Germany's highest peak, where the 1936 Winter Olympics were held. (A look at the ski jump is worthwhile. Note the Aryan (Nazi) carvings.) There's a reason for all the big American cars you're seeing: Garmisch is a major resort for U.S. forces in Europe. From Garmisch, continue south into Austria. At scenic Lermoos, head north for Reutte.

If travelling by train pass, catch the Romantic Road bus tour from the Rothenburg railway station or from the *parkplatz* at the north end of town; two buses come through in the early afternoon. You can catch one bus into Munich (arrives at 18:55) or the other direct to Fussen (arrives at 19:55). Ask about reservations and exact times in Rothenburg at the railway station or tourist office. Be early! If you get a seat when the bus arrives, you'll have a better chance of being on it when it leaves two hours later.

Dachau
Dachau, the first Nazi concentration camp (1933), served as a 'model' for others across Nazi Europe. Today it is the most accessible camp to travellers, and a very effective voice from our recent grisly past, warning and pleading 'Never Again'—the memorial's theme. This is a valuable experience, and when approached thoughtfully is well worth the drive. See it. Feel it. Read about it. Think. After this most powerful sightseeing experience, many people gain a healthy respect for history and are inspired to keep the gap between them and their government manageable. Fascism could recur anywhere. . .

Upon arrival, pick up the mini-guidebook and notice when the next documentary film in English will be shown (normally 11:30, 14:00 and 15:30). The museum and the film are worthwhile. Notice the expressionist Fascist-inspired art near the theatre. Outside, be sure to tour the reconstructed barracks, the crematoriums and memorial shrines at the far end. (Near the theatre are English books, slides and a toilet. The camp is open 9:00-17:00, closed on Mondays.)

Dachau

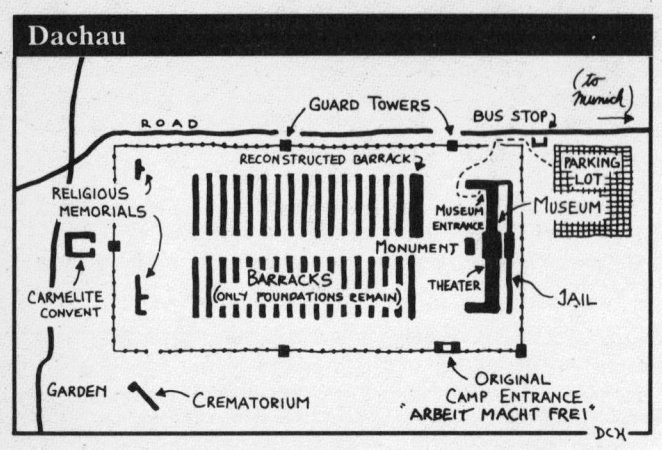

Map labels: Road; Guard Towers; Bus Stop (to Munich); Reconstructed Barrack; Parking Lot; Museum; Museum Entrance; Monument; Theater; Jail; Religious Memorials; Carmelite Convent; Barracks (only foundations remain); Garden; Crematorium; Original Camp Entrance "Arbeit Macht Frei"

Trains go from Munich to the Dachau station regularly, where a public bus to the concentration camp leaves every 45 minutes.

Munich

Marienplatz is the central square of this booming and very human city. An hour strolling around here will give you a taste of the ambience and urban energy of Munich. The city hall on the square, with its famous *glockenspiel* (chime), has a lift for a good city view. Two blocks away is the Hofburg, the old royal palace complex—fine baroque theatre, gardens, palace tour and museum. Also nearby are the bustling outdoor Viktualen Market and the rowdy, famous and touristy beerhall, the Hofbrauhaus. Drop in for lunch and the curious spectacle of 200 Japanese drinking beer in a German beerhall. Or visit the less touristy, more German Mathauser's beerhall at 5 Bayerstrasse between the station and Karlstor.

The Olympic village is a pleasant park with an impressive tower view, giant pool, easy parking and, across the street, the popular BMW factory, museum and tour (the black piston-shaped towers).

Eating and Sleeping

In July and August Munich and Bavaria are packed with tourists. Tyrol in Austria is easier and a bit cheaper. Reutte (pron.: ROY-tuh) is just one of many good places to stay in the area. It's not as crowded as some other towns in peak season, the easy-going locals are always in a party mood, and staying overnight in Austria is fun. Reutte has two great youth hostels. To reach the central hostel (tel. 05672-3039), follow the **Jugendherberg** signs from the town centre (a five-minute walk), look for 'Kindergarten' sign; the hostel accepts non-members, is clean, friendly and rarely full.

Just over the river, one mile from the Reutte station, is Frau Rayman's **Jugendgastehaus am Graben**. (A-6600 Hofen, Reutte in Tirol, tel. 05672/2644); this classy youth hostel, open all year, charges £4.50 (95AS) per person including breakfast, sheets and shower in rooms with two to 12 beds, and serves great dinners for £1.60 (35AS). My favourite hotel in town is the big, central **Hotel Goldener Hirsch** (from Germany dial 0043-5672-2508, in Reutte just the last four digits, ask for Helmut or Monika) which charges £14 (308AS) per person and serves great £4.50 (95AS) dinners. The Reutte tourist office, one block in front of the station, can always find you a £5 (110AS) bed in a private home (open until 18:00 daily, tel. 05672/2336).

In Munich there's a helpful room-finding service in the station's tourist information office (open Mon.-Sat., 8:00-23:00, Sun. 13:00-21:30, tel. 089/2391-256). They can usually find you a reasonable room (£30 (90DM) doubles) near the station. In Oberammergau I enjoyed friendly budget accommodation and hearty cooking at the **Gasthaus zum Stern** (Dorfstrasse 33, 8103 Oberammergau, tel. 08822/867).

Oberammergau's **youth hostel** is modern and decent (tel. 08822/4114). Countryside guest houses abound in Bavaria and are a great value. Look for signs that say '*Zimmer frei*'. The going rate is £15 (46DM) per double including breakfast.

Itinerary Options
To save a day you could see Rothenburg during the Romantic Road tour lunch stop and continue south. Munich is a cultural centre, capital of Bavaria, and is well worth at least a day if you have the time.

Austria

■ 32,000 square miles.
■ 7.6 million people (235 per square mile and holding).
■ During the grand old Hapsburg days, Austria was Europe's most powerful empire. Its royalty put together that giant empire of more than 50 million people by making love, not war (having lots of children and marrying them into the other royal houses of Europe).
■ Today this small landlocked country does more to cling to its elegant past than any other in Europe. The waltz is still the rage, and Austrians are very sociable. More so than anywhere else, it's important to greet people you pass on the streets or meet in shops. The Austrian's version of Hello is a cheerful 'Grüss Gott' ('May God greet you'). You'll get the correct pronunciation after the first volley—listen and copy.

■ Austrian Currency: The Austrian Schilling (S or AS) is divided into 100 Gröschen (g). There are about 22 AS in a pound so each schilling is worth a bit less than 5p. Divide prices by 22 to get costs in pounds. The AS is tied to the DM, 1 DM always equals 7AS.

■ While they speak German, and German currency (coins and paper) is readily accepted in Saltzburg, Innsbruck and Reutte, the Austrians cherish their distinct cultural and historical traditions. They are *not* Germans. Austria is mellow and relaxed compared to Germany. *Gemütlichkeit* is the local word for this special Austrian cosy-and-easy approach to life. It's good living—whether engulfed in mountain beauty or bathed in lavish high culture. The people stroll as if every day were Sunday, topping things off with a visit to a coffee or pastry shop.

■ It must be nice to be past your prime—no longer troubled by being powerful, able to sit back and enjoy just being happy in the clean, untroubled mountain air. While the Austrians make less money than their neighbours, they work less (34 hours a week) and live longer (14 per cent of the people are senior citizens, the highest percentage in the world). Austria is a neutral country and not in NATO or the EEC.

■ Austrians eat at about the same times as we do. Treats include *Wiener Schnitzel* (breaded veal cutlet), *Knödel* (dumplings), *Apfelstrudel* and fancy desserts. Be sure to try *Sachertorte*, a great chocolate cake from Vienna. White wines, Heurigen (new wine) and coffee are delicious and popular. Shops are open from 8:00 to 17:00. Banks keep roughly the same hours, but usually close for lunch.

TOUR 7

BAVARIA AND CASTLE DAY

Our goal on this tour is to explore two very different castles, Germany's finest rococo-style church, and a typical Bavarian village. The thrill for the day is a luge ride—take a ski lift up and zoom down the mountain sitting on an oversized skateboard! The plan is a circular tour through a fascinating bit of southern Germany, starting and ending in the Austrian town of Reutte.

Suggested Schedule

7:30	Breakfast.
8:00	Leave Reutte.
8:30	Neuschwanstein, tour Ludwig's castle.
11:30	Lakeside picnic under the castle.
12:15	Drive to Wies Church (20-minute stop) and on to Oberammergau.
13:45	Tour Oberammergau theatre and town or Linderhof castle.
15:15	Drive back into Austria via Garmisch and the Zugspitze.
16:30	*Sommerrodelbahn* (luge) ride in Lermoos.
18:00	Walk to ruined castle.
19:30	Dinner in Reutte.
20:30	Tyrol folk evening (if not last night).

Transport and Sightseeing Highlights

This day is designed for drivers: without your own wheels it won't all be possible. Local buses serve the area—but not very well. Buses from the Fussen station to Neuschwanstein run hourly and cost 50p (11AS); Fussen-Wies, twice a day for £1.70 (37AS); Oberammergau-Linderhof, fairly regularly. Hitchhiking is possible, but without a car, to cover these sights most efficiently, I'd make my headquarters in Munich and take an all-day bus tour. Or, make Reutte your base and just tour Neuschwanstein, Fussen and the Reutte ruins. Reutte-to-Fussen buses run regularly until about 18:00.

It's best to see Neuschwanstein, Germany's most popular castle, early in the morning before the hordes hit it. The castle is open every morning at 8:30; by 10:00 it's packed. Take the English tour and learn the story of Bavaria's 'Mad' King Ludwig.

After the tour, if you are energetic, climb up to Mary's Bridge for a great view of Europe's 'Fairytale' castle. From the bridge,

Bavaria & Tyrol—The Castle Loop

[Map showing the Castle Loop region with labels: Romantic Road to Rothenburg, Steingaden, Wies, Echelsbacher Bridge (Gorge), Autobahn to Munich, Oberammergau, WEST GERMANY, Forgensee, Tegelberg, Neuschwanstein, Hohenschwangau, Füssen, Alpsee, Ettal, Linderhof, Reutte, Ehrenberg Ruins, Plansee, Garmisch-Partenkirchen, Zugspitze 2973 m, Luge, Lermoos, Luge, Lousy Road!, Great view!, Fernpass, Tunnel to Innsbrück, Fallerschein, AUSTRIA — DCH]

the fit enjoy walking even higher to the 'Beware—Danger of Death' signs and an even more glorious castle view. The big, yellow, more 'lived-in' Hohenschwangau castle nearby was Ludwig's boyhood home. Like its more exciting neighbour, Hohenschwangau costs about £1.50 (30AS) and takes about an hour to tour.

Back down in the village you'll find several restaurants. The Jagerhaus is by far the cheapest, with food that tastes that way. Next door is a handy little family-run grocer's. Picnic in the lakeside park. At the intersection you'll find the best gift shop (with fine manger scenes and Hummels), the bus stop, post office and international dial-direct-to-home phone booths.

Just north of Neuschwanstein is the Tegelberg cable car. For £5.30 (16DM) it will carry you high above the castle to that peak's 5,500-foot summit and back down. On a clear day you get great views of the Alps and Bavaria and the thrill of watching hang-gliders leap into airborne ecstasy. From there it's a lovely two-hour walk to Ludwig's castle. Tegelberg has a mountain hut with Tolkien atmosphere and £3.50 (10DM) beds, in case you'd like to spend the night and see Ludwig's place the next morning. (Last car 17:00.)

Neuschwanstein—'Mad' King Ludwig's Castle

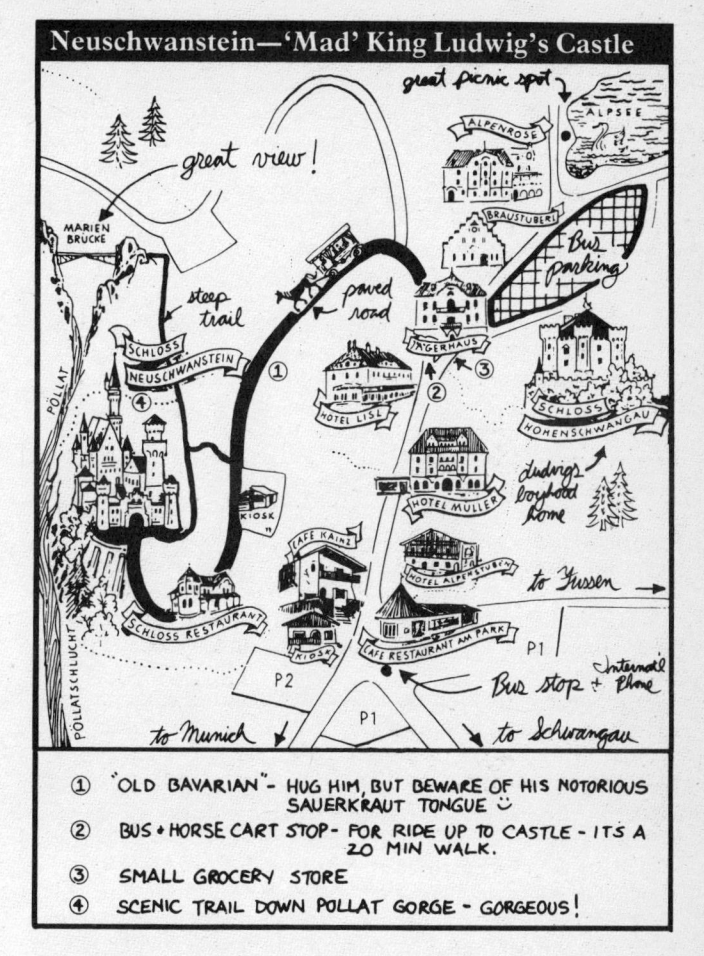

[Hand-drawn map with the following labels: great picnic spot, ALPSEE, ALPENROSE, great view!, MARIEN BRUCKE, BRAUSTUBERL, Bus parking, steep trail, paved road, SCHLOSS NEUSCHWANSTEIN, JÄGERHAUS, ①, ③, HOTEL LISL, SCHLOSS HOHENSCHWANGAU, ④, POLLAT, Ludwig's boyhood home, KIOSK, HOTEL MÜLLER, CAFE KAINZ, HOTEL ALPE STUBEN, to Füssen, SCHLOSS RESTAURANT, POLLATSCHLUCHT, KIOSK, ②, CAFE RESTAURANT AM PARK, P1, Bus stop + International Phone, P2, P1, to Munich, to Schwangau]

① "OLD BAVARIAN" - HUG HIM, BUT BEWARE OF HIS NOTORIOUS SAUERKRAUT TONGUE ☺
② BUS + HORSE CART STOP - FOR RIDE UP TO CASTLE - ITS A 20 MIN WALK.
③ SMALL GROCERY STORE
④ SCENIC TRAIL DOWN POLLAT GORGE - GORGEOUS!

Germany's greatest rococo-style church, Wies Kirche, is bursting with beauty just 30 minutes down the road. Go north, turn right at Steingaden, and follow the signs. This church is a droplet of heaven, a curly curlicue, the final flowering of the baroque movement. Read about it as you sit in its splendour, then walk back the long way, through the meadow, to the car park. (Until 1990, it's being restored, and much of its ornate charm is scaffolded up. Tour Oberammergau's church or the splendid Etal Monastery nearby instead.)

Oberammergau, the Shirley Temple of Bavarian villages and

exploited to the hilt by the tourist trade, has a resilient charm. It's worth a wander. Browse through the woodcarvers' shops—small art galleries filled with very expensive whittled works. Visit the church, a cousin of the Wies. Tour the great Passion Play theatre (in English, 45 minutes long) and get out.

From Oberammergau drive through Garmisch, past Germany's highest mountain, the Zugspitze, into Austria via Lermoos. Or you can take the small scenic road past Ludwig's Linderhof Castle. It's the most liveable place I've seen. Incredible grandeur on a homely scale, and worth a look if you have the energy and two hours for the tour.

The Fernpass road from Reutte to Innsbruck passes the ruined castles of Ehrenberg (just outside town) and two exciting luge courses. The first course is a ten-minute drive beyond the ruins; look for a chairlift on the side of the road. In the summer, this ski slope is used as a luge course, or *sommerrodelbahn*. This is one of Europe's great thrills: take the lift up, grab a sled-like go-cart and luge down. The concrete bobsled course banks on the corners and even a novice can go very, very fast. No one emerges from the course without a windblow hairdo and a smile-creased face. (Closed at 17:00, off-season, and when raining.) Twenty minutes further toward Innsbruck, just past Lermoos at Biberwihr (the first exit after a long tunnel) is a better luge, the longest in Austria—4,000 feet. It opens at 8:30—a good tomorrow morning alternative if today is wet.

The brooding ruins of Ehrenberg await survivors of the luge. These are a great contrast after this morning's 'modern' castles. Park in the car park at the base of the hill and walk up; it's a 20-minute walk to the small castle for a great view from your own private ruins. For more castle mystique, climb 30 minutes more up the taller neighbouring hill. Its ruined castle is bigger, more desolate and overgrown, more romantic. The easiest way down is via the small road from the gulley between the two castles. Reutte is a long but pleasant walk away.

By now it's dinnertime and, if you've done all this, you'll have a good appetite. Ask in your hotel if there's a Tyrolian folk evening tonight. Somewhere in Reutte there should be an evening of yodelling, slap-dancing and Tyrolian frolic—always worth the £2 (50AS) charge.

Itinerary Options
Train travellers may prefer spending this time in Munich and in Saltzburg (two hours apart by hourly train). Salzburg holds its own against 'castle day' and is better than Innsbruck. Consider a side trip to Saltzburg from Munich and the night train from Munich to Venice.

TOUR 8

DRIVE OVER THE ALPS TO VENICE

Innsbruck, western Austria's major city and just a scenic hour's drive from Reutte, is a great place to spend the morning. Park as centrally as possible, and give yourself three hours to see the traffic-free town centre and have a picnic lunch. Then it's on to Italia. Italy is a whole new world—sunshine, cappuccino, *gelato* and *la dolce vita*!

Suggested Schedule

8:00	Drive from Reutte to Innsbruck.
9:30	Sightsee in Innsbruck or tour Reifenstein Castle, lunch.
12:30	Drive from Innsbruck or Reifenstein to Venice.
17:30	Take boat No. 1 (the slow boat) down the Grand Canal to San Marco. Find your hotel.

Transport

From Reutte the scenic highway takes you past ruined castles, two luge courses (the longest one is behind you on the left after the tunnel), over Fernpass and into the valley of the Inn River. To get into Innsbruck, take the 'Innsbruck West' exit, following signs to Brenner Pass and Italy. On the hill just south of Innsbruck you'll see the Olympic ski jump; to visit it, follow 'Bergisel' signs.

The dramatic Brenner Pass motorway sweeps you quickly and effortlessly over the Alps. The famous Europa Bridge comes with a steep toll but saves you enough petrol, time, and nausea to be worthwhile. (Good toilet and picnic spot at the bridge.) About 30 minutes south of Innsbruck is Italy.

In four hours, the *autostrada* zips you through a castle-studded valley past impressive mountains, around Romeo and Juliet's home town of Verona and on into Venice. For the rest of this trip you'll be paying tolls for your motorway driving.

At Venice the motorway ends like Medusa's head. Follow the parking signs. There are three or four car-parks with red or green lights indicating whether or not they have more room; follow the signs to 'Piazza Roma', the most convenient car-park, and choose either the huge cheaper open parking (the vast field to right of bridge) or the safer, more expensive multi-storey car-park right on the square. From there you can visit the tourist information office and catch the boat of your choice deep into Europe's most enchanting city.

Innsbruck

[Map of Innsbruck with the following labels:]

- DOTTED LINE (---) ENCLOSES OLD QUARTER PEDESTRIAN AREA
- TO HAFELEKAR GONDOLA
- ST. JACOB'S CHURCH
- HOFBURG PALACE
- HOFGARTEN PARK
- GOLDEN ROOF & OLYMPIC MUSEUM
- THEATER
- TO MUNICH & VIENNA
- HELBLINGHAUS
- INN RIVER
- TYROLEAN FOLK ART MUSEUM
- ANNA'S COLUMN
- CITY TOWER
- POST OFFICE
- TRAIN STATION
- TRIUMPHAL ARCH
- TO VENICE & ROME
- TO BERGISEL SKI JUMP

—DCH—

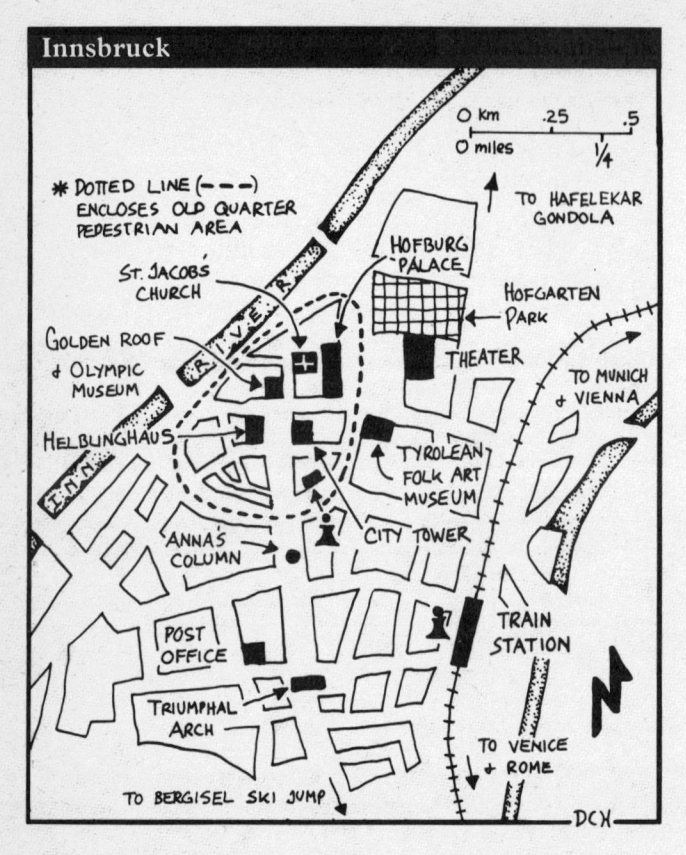

By train it's 2½ hours from Reutte to Innsbruck and six hours from there to Venice. It's best to take the overnight train from Munich or Innsbruck direct to Venice. The train drops you at the edge of Venice, where you'll find a helpful tourist information office with maps and a room-finding service. In front of the station is the boat dock where the floating 'city buses' (*vaporetti*) stop.

Sightseeing Highlights

●●**Innsbruck**—The Golden Roof (*Goldenes Dachl*) is the historic centre of town. In this square you'll see a tourist information booth with maps and lists of sights, the newly restored baroque-style Helblinghaus, the city tower (climb it for a great view), and the new Olympics museum with exciting action videos for winter-sports lovers.

Nearby are the palace (Hofburg) and church and the unique

Tiroler Volkskunst Museum. This museum (85p (19AS), open
9:00-17:00 daily, closed Sunday afternoons) is the best look
anywhere at traditional Tyrolian lifestyles. Fascinating exhibits
range from wedding dresses and babies' cribs to nativity scenes.
Use the helpful English guidebook (£1.50 (35AS)).

A very popular mountain sports centre and home of the 1964 and
1976 Winter Olympics, Innsbruck is surrounded by 150 mountain
lifts, 1,250 miles of trails and 250 climbers' huts. If it's sunny,
consider taking the Hafelekar lift right out of the city to the
mountaintops above (£10.50 (230AS)).

The quickest way to 'see' Innsbruck is to make a short stop at
the Olympic ski jump (*bergisel*) just off the road as you head south.
Climb to the Olympic rings eternal flame holder and enjoy the
commanding view.

● ●**Reifenstein Castle**—For one of Europe's most intimate looks
at medieval castle life, let the lady of Reifenstein show you around
her wonderfully preserved castle. She leads tours on the hour
in Italian and German. She's friendly and will squeeze in what
English she can.

Just inside Italy, leave the *autostrada* at Vipiteno/Sterzing
(the town, like many in this area, has both a German and an Italian
name) and drive to the base of the castle's rock. Telephone
0472/765879 in advance to confirm your tour. The pleasant
mini-park beside the drawbridge is a good spot for a picnic. (Be
sure to pick up your litter.) Closed 12:00-14:00.

Italy

■ 116,000 square miles.
■ 56,000,000 people (477 per square mile).
■ Ah, Italy! It has Europe's richest, craziest culture—if I had
to choose just one, Italy's my favourite. Italy is wonderful, if you
take it on its terms and acccept the package deal. Some people,
often with considerable effort, manage to hate it. Italy bubbles with
emotion, corruption, stray hairs, inflation, traffic jams, body odour,
strikes, rallies, holidays, crowded squalor, and irate ranters shaking
their fists at each other one minute and walking arm in arm
the next. Have a talk with yourself before you cross the border.
Promise yourself to relax, and soak in it: it's a glorious mud
puddle. Be militantly positive.

■ With so much history and art in Venice, Florence and Rome,
you'll need to be a student here to maximise your experience.
There are two Italys: the north is relatively industrial, aggressive
and 'time-is-money' in its outlook. The Po River basin and the area
between Milan, Genoa and Turin is the richest farmland and
the industrial heartland. The south is more crowded, poor, relaxed,

farm-oriented and traditional. Families here are very strong and usually live in the same house for many generations. Loyalties are to the family, city, region, then country—in that order. The Appenine Mountains give Italy a rugged north-south spine.

■ Economically, Italy has its problems but things somehow work out. Statistically it looks terrible (high inflation, low average income) but things work wonderfully under the table. Italy is a leading wine producer and is sixth in the world in cheese and wool output. Tourism is a big part of the economy.

■ Italy, home of the Vatican, is Catholic but the dominant religion is football—especially since their 1982 World Cup victory.

■ The language is easy. Be melodramatic and move your hand with your tongue. Hear the melody, get into the flow. Make it up as you go along; Italians are outgoing characters; they want to communicate, and try harder than any other Europeans: play with them.

■ Italy, a land of extremes, is also the most thief-ridden country you'll visit. Tourists suffer virtually no violent crime—just petty purse-snatchings, pick-pocketings and short-changings. Only the sloppy will be stung. Wear your money-belt!

■ Traditionally, Italy uses the siesta plan: people work from 8:00 or 9:00 to 13:00 and from 15:30 to 19:00, six days a week. Many businesses have adopted the government's new recommended

8:00-14:00 work day. In tourist areas, shops are open longer.
■ Sightseeing hours are always changing in Italy and many of the hours in this book will be wrong by the time you travel. Use the local tourist offices to double-check your sightseeing plans.
■ For extra sightseeing information, take advantage of the cheap, colourful, poorly written but informative city guidebooks sold on the streets all over. Also, take advantage of the information telephones you'll find in most historic buildings. Just set the dial on English, pop in your coins and listen. The narration is often accompanied by a mini-slide show. Many dark interiors can be brilliantly lit for a few pence. Whenever possible, let there be light.
■ Some important Italian churches require modest dress—no shorts or bare shoulders.
■ The Italian *autostrada* is lined with some of Europe's best service areas, with petrol, coffee bars, toilets, international telephones, grocery shops, restaurants and often change facilities and tourist info.
■ While no longer a cheap country, Italy is still a hit with shoppers. Glassware (Venice), gold, silver, leather and prints (Florence) and high fashion (Rome) are good souvenirs.
■ Many tourists are mind-boggled by the huge price figures: 16,000 lire (L) for dinner! 42,000 for the room! 126,000 for the taxi! That's still *real* money—it's just spoken of in much smaller units then a pound. Since there are roughly 2,300 L in a pound, work out Italian prices by covering the last three zeros with your finger and more or less halving the remaining figure. That 16,000 L dinner costs £7, the 42,000 L room—£18, and the taxi. . .oh-oh!
■ Beware of the 'slow count'. After you buy something you may get your change back very slowly, one note at a time. The salesperson (or bank teller) hopes you are confused by all the zeros and will gather up your money and say *grazie* before he finishes the count. Always do your own counting and understand the transaction. Only the sloppy are ripped off.
■ Italians eat a miniscule breakfast, a huge lunch between 12:30 and 15:30, and a light dinner quite late. Food in Italy is given great importance and should be thought of as 'sightseeing for your tongue'. Focus on regional specialities, wines and pastas. In restaurants you'll be charged a cover charge (*coperto*) and a 10-15% service charge. A salad, minestrone and pasta, while not a proper meal, is cheap, fun and satisfying. *Gelati* (ice cream) and coffee are art forms in Italy. Have fun in the bars, explore the menus. Bar procedure can be frustrating. Decide what you want, check the price list on the wall, pay the cashier, give the receipt to the barman and tell him what you want.

The Venice Lagoon

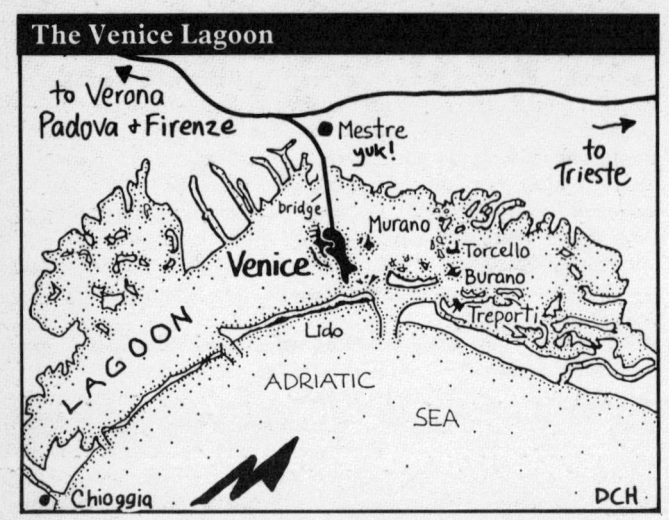

Map showing the Venice Lagoon with labels: to Verona Padova & Firenze, Mestre yuk!, bridge, Venice, Murano, Torcello, Burano, Treporti, to Trieste, Lido, LAGOON, ADRIATIC SEA, Chioggia. Signed DCH.

■ *Il Dolce Far Niente* (the sweetness of doing nothing) is a big part of Italy. Zero in on the fine points. Don't dwell on the problems, accept Italy as a package deal. Savour your cappuccino, dangle your feet over a canal (if it smells, breathe with your mouth) and imagine what it was like centuries ago. Look into the famous sculpted eyes of Michelangelo's David, and understand Renaissance man's assertion of himself. Ramble through the rubble of Rome and mentally resurrect those ancient stones. Sit silently on a hilltop rooftop. Get chummy with the winds of the past. Write a poem over a glass of local wine in a sun-splashed, wave-dashed Riviera village. For romantics, Italy is magic.

Venice Orientation and Arrival

The island city of Venice is shaped like a fish. Its major thoroughfares are canals. The Grand Canal snakes through the middle of the fish starting at the mouth, where all cars, trains, people and food enter, passing under the Rialto Bridge and ending at St. Mark's Square. Only three bridges cross the Grand Canal, but several *traghetti* (little ferry gondolas) shuttle smart walkers across the canal where necessary.

The city has no real streets, and addresses are hopelessly confusing. There are six districts, each with about 6,000 address numbers. Navigate by landmarks, not streets. Luckily, it's fairly easy to find your way, since nearly every street corner has a sign pointing you to the nearest major landmark (San Marco, Rialto, etc.) and most hotels and restaurants have district maps on their cards. (If you get lost, they love to hand them out to prospective customers.)

It's worth buying a cheap little Venice guidebook with a city map and explanation of the major sights at a souvenir stand when you arrive. Most people who have anything to sell to tourists (beds, meals, souvenirs) speak some English.

The public transport system is a fleet of bus-boats called *vaporetti*. They work just like normal city buses except that they float, the stops are docks, and if you get off between stops you may drown. A journey costs about 65p (1500L). Any city map shows the boat stops and routes. Buy your ticket at the ticket window (and count your change). Boat No. 1 is the slow boat down the Grand Canal, No. 2 is the fast way to cut across to St. Mark's. Boat No. 5 gives you an interesting circular tour of the city.

If you've never been there, Venice is confusing. (Even if you have been there, it can be confusing.) It's a car-less kaleidoscope of people, bridges and canals. Venice is like no other city. Don't miss it.

Tourist information offices are located at Piazza Roma (tel. 5227402) where you'll park your car; at the station (tel. 715016); and at St. Mark's Square (tel. 5226356). They are open from 8:30 to 19:30. The offices at the car-park and station are basically room-finding services. The office at St. Mark's is best for confirming your sightseeing plans—they have the latest museum hours listed. Budget travellers, ask for the booklet 'Venezia in Jeans' 40p (1000L).

Accept the fact that Venice was a tourist town 200 years ago. It was, is and always will be crowded. The crowds and tacky souvenir stalls vanish when you hit the back streets.

Eating and Sleeping

Venice is a notoriously difficult place to find a room. You can minimise problems by (1) phoning ahead to make a reservation, (2) travelling out of season, (3) arriving very early—as you will if you take an overnight train from Munich, Vienna or Rome, (4) staying in a mainland town nearby and sidetripping to Venice (Padua, just 30 minutes away by train, is best), or (5) using the tourist information office's room-finding service. Phoning ahead is the best approach.

I stay at the **Locanda Sturion** (S. Polo, Rialto, Calle Sturion 679, 30125 Venezia, tel. 5236243; from Austria or Germany dial 0039/41/5236243). Sergio and Sandro speak good English (normally in from 8:00 to 11:00) and will hold a room until 16:00 with no deposit. Their hotel is 500 years old, located 100 yards from the Rialto Bridge, opposite the boat dock. Doubles cost £23 (53,000L).

Venezia/Venice

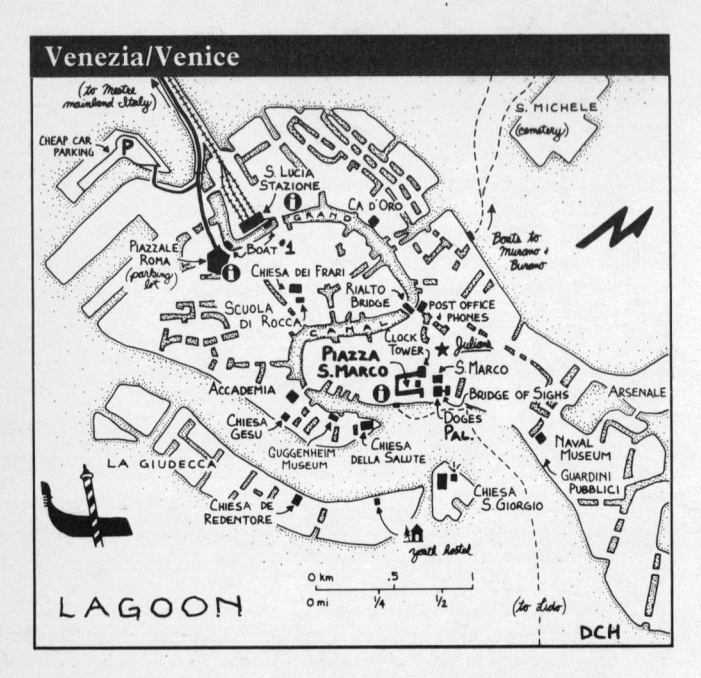

Another good bet is the **Locanda Casa Petrarca**, Calle Schiavine 4386, near San Marco, two blocks south of Campo San Lucco just off Calle dei Fuseri (tel. 5200430; Nelli speaks English, £23 (53,000L) doubles). **Locanda Silva** (tel. 5227643; follow Calle dell' Angelo from San Marco, take the second right across the bridge; left from Fondamenta del Rimedio) is clean and pleasant, located right on a peaceful canal, £22 (50,000L) doubles with shower and breakfast. More expensive and closer to San Marco is **Hotel Città di Milano** (200 yards north of the church, tel. 5227002).

The Venice **youth hostel** (on Giudecca Island, tel. 5238211, 'Zittele' stop on boat No. 5 or No. 8) is crowded, clean, cheap and efficient. Their budget cafeteria welcomes non-hostelers. Each summer the city uses a few schools to house budget travellers with sleeping bags. The tourist office has a list of these very cheap options.

Three of my favourite restaurants are: **Rosticceria San Bartolomeo** at Calle della Bissa 5424, near the Rialto Bridge, just off Campo San Bartolomeo (a busy, cheap, and confusing self-service restaurant on the ground floor, great budget meals in full-service restaurant upstairs, tel. 5223569, open 10:00-14:30, 17:00-21:00, closed Mon.); **Trattoria de Remigio** (Castello 3416, tel. 5230089, make a reservation; this popular place is wonderfully 'local' and in a great area for after-meal wandering); **Trattoria Dona Onesta** (3922 Dorsoduro, tel 5229586) is a fun working class eatery serving cheap and good lunches and dinners near the Cà Foscari. Also near the Cà Foscari is the **University Mensa** (cafeteria). Tourists are welcome (summer only), good atmosphere, £3 (7,000L) meals, third floor above the fire department boats.

For low-stress budget meals, you'll find plenty of self-service restaurants ('self-service' in Italian). One is right at the Rialto Bridge. The **Wendy's** just off San Marco on Calle Larga San Marco serves an all-you-can-eat salad bar for £2.50 (6,000L). Another budget-saver is bar snacks. You'll find plenty of stand-up mini-meals in out-of-the-way bars. Order by pointing. (See tomorrow's pub-crawl.)

TOUR 9
VENICE

Soak in this puddle of elegant decay all day long. Venice is Europe's best-preserved big city. This car-free urban wonderland consists of more than one hundred islands, laced together by nearly five hundred bridges. Born in a lagoon 1,500 years ago as a refuge from barbarians, Venice is overloaded with tourists and slowly sinking (two unrelated facts). In the Middle Ages, after the Venetians created a great trading empire, they smuggled in the bones of St. Mark (San Marco) and Venice gained religious importance as well. Venice has so much to offer and is worth at least a day on even the speediest tour. I am suggesting two nights and a day.

Suggested Schedule

8:00	Breakfast, banking.
9:00	Basilica dei Frari and/or Scuola di San Rocco—for art lovers—or free to browse and shop.
11:00	Visit Accademia Gallery.
12:30	Lunch, canal-side picnic?
14:00	St. Mark's area—tour Doge's Palace, Basilica, take lift to top of Campanile, glass-blowing demonstration.
17:30	Siesta in hotel.
19:00	Dinner or commence pub crawl.

Sightseeing Highlights

●●●**Take the *Vaporetti*—**Venice's floating buses take you anywhere in town for 65p (1500L). Boat No. 1 is the slow boat down the Grand Canal (for the best do-it-yourself introductory tour). No. 5 offers a circular tour of the city (get off at Murano for glass-blowing). There are plenty of boats leaving from San Marco to the beach (Lido), as well as speedboat tours of Burano (a quiet, picturesque fishing and lace town), to Murano (glass-blowing island) and to Torcello (oldest churches and mosaics on an otherwise desolate island).

●●●**Doge's Palace (Palazzo Ducale)—**The former ruling palace has the second largest wooden room in Europe, virtually wallpapered by Tintoretto, Veronese and other great painters. The attached Bridge of Sighs leads to the prison (open 8:30-19:00, £2.20 (5,000L)). No tours: buy a guidebook in the street.

Tour 9

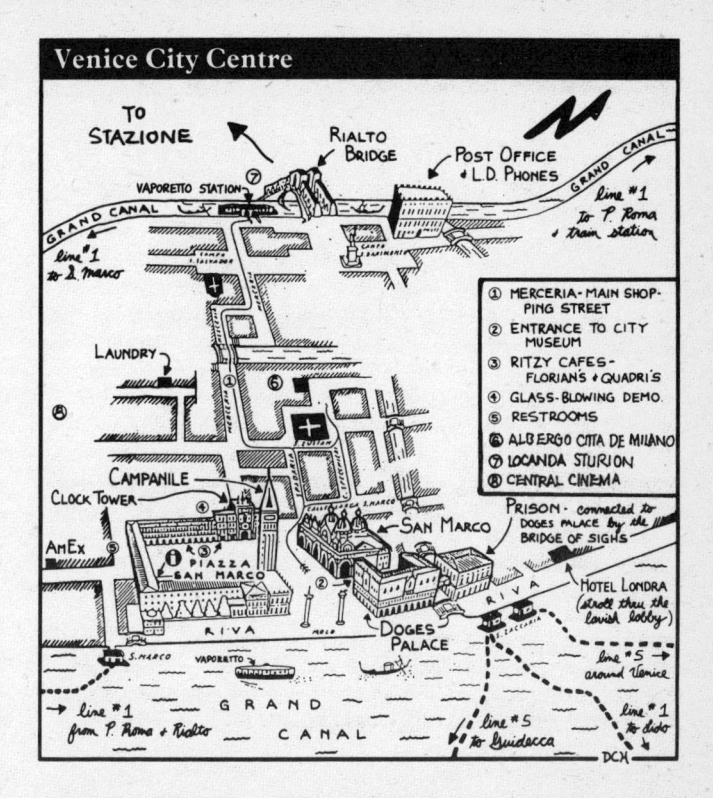

Venice City Centre

(map of Venice city centre showing Grand Canal, Rialto Bridge, Stazione, Post Office & L.D. Phones, Vaporetto Station, Laundry, Campanile, Clock Tower, AmEx, Piazza San Marco, San Marco, Doges Palace, Prison, Bridge of Sighs, Hotel Londra, vaporetto lines #1 and #5)

Map legend:
① MERCERIA – MAIN SHOPPING STREET
② ENTRANCE TO CITY MUSEUM
③ RITZY CAFES – FLORIAN'S + QUADRI'S
④ GLASS-BLOWING DEMO.
⑤ RESTROOMS
⑥ ALBERGO CITTA DE MILANO
⑦ LOCANDA STURION
⑧ CENTRAL CINEMA

●●●**St. Mark's Basilica**—For 1,100 years it has housed the saint's bones. Study the ceiling mosaics, the floor, treasures, the newly restored bronze horses upstairs, and views from the balcony. Modest dress (no shorts) usually required. (Open 9:30-17:30, free, tel. 5200333 for info on free guided tours of the church.)

●●**Campanile di San Marco**—Take the lift (65p (1500L)) up 300 feet to the top of the bell tower for the best possible view of Venice. Notice photos on wall inside showing how this bell tower crumbled into a pile of individual bricks in 1902, 1,000 years after it was built. Be on top when the bells ring for a most ear-shattering experience (ask about times). Open 9:30-22:30.

Clock Tower—See the bronze men (Moors) in action. Open 9:00-12:00 and 15:00-17:00, £1 (2500L). Notice the world's first 'digital' clock on the tower facing St. Mark's Square.

●●**Gallerie dell' Accademia**—Venice's top art museum is packed with the painted highlights of the Venetian Renaissance. (Bellini, Giorgione, Veronese, Tiepolo, Canaletto, etc.) Just over the wooden Accademia Bridge. Open 9:00-19:00, Sun. 9:00-13:00, closed Mondays. £1.75 (4,000L).

- **Chiesa dei Frari**—A great church houses Donatello's woodcarving of St. John the Baptist, a Bellini, Titian's Assumption and much more. Open 9:00-noon, 14:30-17:30.
- **Scuola di San Rocco**—Next to the Frari church, another lavish building bursts with art, including some 50 Tintorettos. View the splendid ceiling paintings with the mirrors available at the entrance. Open 9:00-13:00, 15:30-18:30, last entrance half an hour before closing, £2.20 (5,000L).

Peggy Guggenheim Collection—A popular collection of way-out art that so many try so hard to understand, it includes works by Picasso, Chagall and Dali. Open noon-18:00, closed Tuesdays, £2 (5,000L); Sat. 18:00-21:00, free. Also, for modern art fans: on even years, Venice hosts the 'World Fair' of art, the Biennale, at the fairgrounds on Venice's 'tail' (*Vaporetto*: 'Biennale').

Gondola Trips—This tradition is a must for many, but a rip-off for most. Gondoliers charge about £30 (70,000L) for a 40-minute ride. You can divide the cost—and the romance—by up to seven people. For cheap gondola thrills, stick to the 15p (300L) one-minute ferry ride on the Grand Canal *traghetti*.

The Venice Experience—For a cool, comfortable bit of sit-down entertainment, see the story-of-Venice film which is shown hourly in the Cinema Centrale, on Piscina di Frezzeria, just behind St. Mark's Square. Ask for directions at the tourist office on the square (corner opposite the church). Good discount for groups of ten or more. Tel. 5794000.

Glass Blowing—It's unnecessary to go all the way to Murano Island to see glass-blowing demonstrations. Hang out in the alley just 20 yards north of St. Mark's Square and follow any tour group into the glass factory outlets for a fun and free ten-minute show.

Evening: The Stand-up Progressive Venetian Pub Crawl Dinner—Venice's residential back streets hide plenty of characteristic bars with plenty of interesting toothpick munchie food. This is a great way to mingle and have fun with the Venetians. The best pubs are in the Castello district near the Arsenal and around the Campo di Formosa.

Find Campo Santa Maria di Formosa. Start with a pizza on the square (at the pizzeria opposite the canal) and ask for Gigi's bar, one block away. Wander the area for a few more bars. Finish with *gelato* by the canal on the other side of Campo di Formosa. Italian hors d'oeuvres wait under glass in every bar; try fried mozzarella cheese, blue cheese, calamari, artichoke hearts and anything ugly on a toothpick. Drink the house wines. When you're ready, ask for a glass of *grappa*. Bars don't stay open very late so start your evening by 19:00. Ask your hotel manager for advice—or to join you.

The snack bar Caffè Cavallo in Piazza S. Giovanni e Paolo serves great lasagna in a quiet square, just past Santa Maria di Formosa.

Night time is the right time in Venice. Soft summer nights, live music, floodlit history and a ceiling of stars make St. Mark's magic at midnight. Shine with the old lanterns on the gondola piers where the sloppy grand Canal splashes at the Doge's Palace. Howl at the moon. Dance with your shadow.

Helpful Hints

Venetian churches and museums keep erratic hours. To minimise frustration, call in at the tourist office on the far corner of St. Mark's Square and pick up the xeroxed sheet with the up-to-date listings of all hours and admission fees.

About wandering in Venice: walk and walk to the far reaches of the town. Don't worry about getting lost: get as lost as possible. Keep reminding yourself, 'I'm on an island and I can't get off.' When the time comes to find your way, just follow those directional arrows on building corners, or simply ask a local, '*Dov'è* (DOH-vay) *San Marco?*' (Where is St. Mark's?).

Try a siesta in the Giardini Publici (public gardens, in the tail area), on the Isle of Burano, or in your hotel.

The best shopping area is around the Rialto Bridge and along the Merceria, the road connecting St. Mark's and the Rialto. Things are cheaper on the non-San Marco side of the Rialto bridge.

If bombed by a pigeon, resist the initial response to wipe it off immediately—it'll just smear into your hair. Wait till it dries, then it will flake off cleanly.

TOUR 10

VENICE—FLORENCE

Leave the splash and flash of Venice for the noble art capital of Europe, Florence. While Florence can't be seen in 24 hours, if you're well-organised you can enjoy the highlights. After the three-hour trip south, get settled, have a siesta, and you'll be ready for a look at the greatest collection of Italian Renaissance paintings and a thrilling walk through the historic centre of the birthplace of the Renaissance.

Suggested Schedule

8:00	Leave Venice.
12:00	Arrive in Florence, check in, siesta.
15:00	Tour Uffizi Gallery for a look at Italy's best paintings.
17:00	Walk through Renaissance core of Firenze.
20:00	Dinner.

Transport

By car, travelling from Venezia (Venice) to Firenze (Florence) is quite easy. It's *autostrada* (with reasonable tolls) all the way. From Venice, follow the signs to Bologna and then head for Firenze. Take the 'Firenze Nord—Al Mare' exit. (The modern church at this exit, dedicated to the workers who lost their lives building this *autostrada*, is worth a look.) Follow signs to 'Centro' and 'Fortezza di Basso'. Parking in Florence is horrendous at best. Get near the *centro* and park where you can.

By train, things are much easier. The Venice-Florence (and Florence-Rome) trains are fast (four hours) and frequent, zipping you into the centrally located station (five-minute walk from *Duomo*). Use train time to eat, study and plan.

Orientation

The hurried tourist sees Florence as an overpriced traffic jam of impersonal too-big buildings, too-small pavements, noisy-nervy drivers and obligatory cultural sights. With the luxury of time, the visitor who gets away from the required sights to browse, eat and snoop in the far corners of the old town will understand the soul of Florence. But for a short stay like ours, it's basically a treasure chest of artistic and cultural wonders from the birthplace of our modern world. We'll get intimate with Italy later in the hill villages

of Umbria and the salty ports of the Riviera. In Florence, it's
a 'supermarket sweep' and the groceries are the best art in Europe.

The Florence we're interested in lies mostly on the north bank
of the Arno River. Nothing is more than a 20-minute walk from the
station, cathedral or Ponte Vecchio (old bridge). While nearly
all the art treasures are on the north side of the river, I choose to
sleep and eat on the more colourful, less awesome, more personal
Oltrarno (south bank).

Arrival: The station is very central, with a handy tourist
information centre and plenty of full-by-early-afternoon reasonable
hotels nearby. Those arriving by car with a hotel reservation can
make life a little easier by driving as close to the centre as possible
and hiring a taxi to lead them to their hotel.

Tourist Offices: Normally overcrowded and understaffed, they
are still important. Pick up a current list of museum hours, confirm
your sightseeing plans and ask for accommodation help. You'll
find small temporary information booths around the town and the
main *Informazione Turistica* at the station (open daily in summer
from 9:00-21:00). The two room-finding services in the station,
ACISJF (30 yards down platform 16, open Mon.-Sat. 10:00-16:00,
closed August, best for budget rooms) and *Informazione Turistiche
Alberghiere* (near platform 10, daily 8:00-21:30, out of season
shorter hours), are your best bets for help in this crowded city.

Florence requires organisation, especially for a blitz tour.
Remember that some attractions close early, while others are open
all day. Everything is within walking distance of the station and the
town centre.

If you arrive early enough, see everyone's essential sight, David,
straight away. In Italy, a masterpiece at hand is worth two down
the street; you never know when a place will unexpectedly lock up.
Otherwise, head for the Uffizi Gallery near the river—late
afternoon is the best time to miss the crowds in this popular
museum.

For a walk through the core of Renaissance Florence, start
at the Accademia (home of Michelangelo's masterpiece, David), and
cut through the heart of the city to the Ponte Vecchio (old bridge)
on the Arno River. (Note: A 20-page self-guided tour of this
walk is outlined in *Mona Winks*. You could do this walk backwards,
starting at the Uffizi and ending at the Accademia.) From the
Accademia, walk down the street to the Cathedral (*Duomo*). See the
famous doors and the interior of the Baptistry. Farther down
that street, notice the statues on the exterior of the Orsanmichele
church and grab a quick lunch nearby. At the end of the street are
the central square (Piazza della Signoria), the city palace (Palazzo
Vecchio) and the great Uffizi Gallery—all very important.

Firenze/Florence

[Map of Florence with handwritten annotations including: (to Rome & Venice), FORTRESS, STAZIONE, S. MARCO, ACCADEMIA (DAVID), MEDICI CHAPEL, STREET MARKET, S. MARIA NOVELLA, "DOWNTOWN" shops, tranks & gelati, BAPTISTERY, DUOMO, DUOMO MUSEUM, ORSANMICHELE, CAMPANILE, Vivoli's GELATI!, PIAZZA DELLA SIGNORIA, BARGELLO, PALAZZO VECCHIO, MICHAELANGELO'S HOUSE, S. CROCE, UFFIZI, PAZZI CHAPEL, leather school, S. SPIRITO, PONTE VECCHIO, RIVER, PITTI PALACE, BOBOLI GARDENS, BELVEDERE FORTRESS, S. MINIATO AL MONTE, PIAZZALE MICHALANGELO (Best view of Firenze).

① VIA CALZAIUOLI - MAIN STREET CAFES, GELATI, SHOPS
② GOOD BOOK + CARDSHOP W/ MONEY EXCHANGE + LONG HRS.
③ PENSION SORELLE BANDINI

—DCH

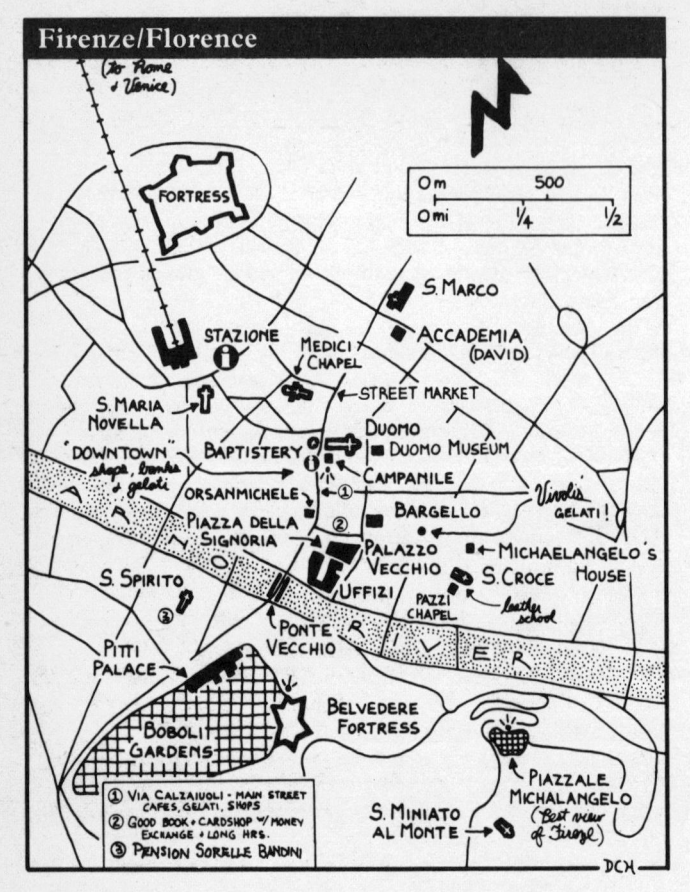

After you walk past the statues of the great men of the Renaissance in the Uffizi courtyard, you'll get to the Arno River and the Ponte Vecchio. Your introductory walk will be over, but your Florence experience will have just begun. After the overview, you'll know what sights to concentrate on tomorrow. You still have half a day to see a lifetime of art and history—or just to shop, people-watch and enjoy Europe's greatest ice cream. Here are a few ideas:

Sightseeing Highlights
●●● **The Accademia (Galleria dell' Accademia)**—Houses Michelangelo's David and his powerful (unfinished) Prisoners. Eavesdrop as tour guides explain these masterpieces. There's also a

lovely Botticelli painting. The newly opened second floor is
worth a quick look for its beautiful pre-Renaissance paintings.
(Open Tues.-Sat. 9:00-14:00, Sun. 9:00-13:00, closed Monday,
£1.75 (4,000L).) Be careful: most Italian museums shut their ticket
windows 30 minutes before closing. There's a great book-and-poster
shop across the street; the chubby £2.50 (6,000L) Florence
book is my choice. Behind the Accademia are the Piazza Santissima
Annunziata with its lovely Renaissance harmony, and the Hospital
of the Innocents (*Spedale degli Innocenti*) by Brunelleschi with
terracotta medallions by della Robbia—often considered the first
Renaissance building (1420s).

● **Museum of San Marco**—One block north of the Accademia on
Piazza San Marco, this museum houses the greatest collection
anywhere of dreamy medieval frescos and paintings by the pre-
Renaissance master, Fra Angelico. You'll see why he thought of his
painting as a form of prayer and couldn't paint a crucifix without
shedding tears. Also see Savonarola's monastic cell. Each of the
monks' cells has a Fra Angelico fresco. Tues.-Sat. 9:00-14:00, Sun.
9:00-13:00, closed Monday.

● ● **The Duomo**—The cathedral of Florence is a mediocre
Gothic building, without much to see on the inside, capped by a
magnificent Renaissance dome—the first Renaissance dome, by
Brunelleschi, and the model for domes to follow. (When working
on St. Peter's in Rome, Michelangelo said, 'I can build
a dome bigger but not more beautiful than the dome of Florence.')
You can climb to the top, but I recommend climbing Giotto's
Tower (*Campanile*) next to it—faster, not so crowded and
with a better view (including the dome). The church's neo-Gothic
facade is from the 1870s, covered with pink, green and
white marble from Tuscany. The tower is open 9:00-19:00 (£1.30
(3,000L)).

● ● **Museo dell' Opera del Duomo**—Cathedral Museum, just
behind the church at No. 9, has many Donatello statues and
a Michelangelo Pietà. Great if you like sculpture. (Mon.-Sat. 9:00-
20:00—maybe earlier, Sun. 10:00-13:00. £1.30 (3,000L)). This is
one of the few museums in Florence that stays open late.

● ● **The Baptistry**—Michelangelo said its bronze doors were fit to
be the 'gates of paradise'. Look for the famous carved bronze
doors (facing the Duomo and around to the right) by Ghiberti—a
breakthrough in perspective, using mathematical laws to create the
illusion of 3-D on a 2-D surface. Go inside Florence's oldest
building for the medieval mosaic ceiling. Compare that to the 'new
improved' art of the Renaissance. (9:30-12:15, 14:30-17:15, free.
Bronze doors always 'open'.)

Orsanmichele—Mirroring Florentine values, it was a combination
church-granary. Pay for a light to get a good look at the glorious

tabernacle. Notice the spouts for grain to pour through the pillars
inside. Go upstairs for the temporary exhibit and a fine city
view (free). Also study the sculpture on its outside walls. You can
see man literally stepping out in the great Renaissance sculptor
Donatello's St. George. (7:00-12:00, 14:00-19:00, free.)
- **Palazzo Vecchio**—The interior of the fortified palace of the
Medici family is interesting only if you're a real Florentine history
fan. Open 9:00-19:00. Michelangelo's David originally stood at
the entrance, where the copy is today. Notice the bronze statue of
Perseus by Cellini in the nearby Loggia.
- - - **Uffizi Gallery**—The greatest collection of Italian painting
anywhere is a must with plenty of works by Giotto, Leonardo,
Raphael, Caravaggio, Rubens, Titian, Michelangelo, and a roomful
of Botticellis. There are no tours, so buy a book in the street
before entering (or follow *Mona Winks*). The museum is nowhere
near as big as it is great: few tourists spend more than two hours
inside. The paintings are wonderfully displayed on one comfortable
floor in chronological order from the 13th through to the 17th
centuries. Good view of the Arno River. (Open 9:00-19:00; Sun.
9:00-13:00; closed Monday, £4 (9,000L).) Enjoy the Uffizi square,
full of artists and souvenir stalls. All the surrounding statues
of the earth-shaking Florentines of 500 years ago remind us that the
Florentine Renaissance was much more than just visual arts.
- - **Bargello (Museo Nazionale)**—The city's greatest sculpture
museum is just behind the Palazzo Vecchio (a five-minute walk
from Uffizi) in a former prison that looks like a mini-Palazzo
Vecchio. Donatello's David, works by Michelangelo, much more.
Very underrated. Open 9:00-14:00, Sun. 9:00-13:00, closed
Monday. (Dante's house is just around the corner.)
- **Medici Chapel (Cappelle dei Medici)**—This chapel is
drenched in incredibly lavish High Renaissance architecture
and sculpture by Michelangelo. Open 9:00-14:00, Sun. 9:00-13:00,
closed Mon.; £2 (4,500L). It's surrounded by a lively market scene
which, for some reason, I find more interesting.
- **Science Museum**—This is a fascinating collection of
Renaissance and later clocks, telescopes, maps and ingenious
gadgets. Also, you can see Galileo's finger in a little shrine-
like bottle. English guidebooklets are available. It's friendly,
comfortably cool, never crowded, and just upstream from the
Uffizi.
- **Michelangelo's Home**—Fans will enjoy his house at Via
Ghibellina 70. 9:00-14:00, closed Tues., £1.75 (4,000L).
- **The Pitti Palace**—Across the river, it has a giant art
collection with works of the masters, plus more modern Italian art
(lovely) and the huge landscaped Boboli Gardens—a cool refuge

from the city heat. (Five museums, 9:00-14:00, Sun. 9:00-13:00,
closed Monday.)

● **Piazzale Michelangelo**—Across the river overlooking the city
(look for the huge statue of David), this square is worth the
half-hour walk or the drive for the view. Just beyond it is the lovely
little San Miniato church. (Bus No. 13 from the station.)

● ● ● *Gelato*—Gelato is a great Florentineedible art form. Italy's
best ice cream is in Florence, especially at Vivoli's in Via Stinche
(see map). Festival del Gelato and Perchè Non, both just off
the pedestrian street running from the *duomo* to the Uffizi, are also
good. That's one souvenir that can't break and won't clutter your
luggage.

There's much, much more. Buy a guidebook. Double check
your plans with the tourist office. Remember, many museums call
it a day at 14:00 and let no one in after 30 minutes before closing.
Most are closed Monday, and at 13:00 on Sunday.

The best views of Florence are from Piazzale Michelangelo from
the top of the *duomo* or Giotto's Tower, and in the poster and card
shops.

Shopping
Florence is a great shopping town. Busy street scenes and markets
abound (especially San Lorenzo, the Mercato Nuovo, on the bridge,
and near Santa Croce). Leather, gold, silver, art prints and tacky
plaster 'mini-Davids' are most popular. Visit the leather school in
the Santa Croce church, inside on the right.

Eating and Sleeping
When it comes to finding a bed, Florence is one of Europe's most
crowded, difficult and overpriced cities. Phone ahead or arrive early
and take advantage of the room-finding services at the station. If
you arrive by early afternoon without a reservation, you can usually
find a reasonable room around the station. The most pleasant
area is in or near Piazza Santa Maria Novella (behind the church,
which is directly in front of the station) and in neighbouring Via
della Scala. Four blocks northeast of the station is the small, clean,
family-run **Casa Rabatti** (Via San Zandei 48, 50129 Florence, tel.
055/212393, £8.50 (20,000L) per person in doubles or quads).

My favourite area is across the river in the Oltrarno area
between the Pitti Palace and the Ponte Vecchio. I stay at **Pensione
Sorelle Bandini**, a 500-year-old palace on a scruffy square, two
blocks from the Pitti Palace just across the old bridge (wonderful
balcony lounge-loggia). Luigi, an American art student who's
adopted Florence, will hold a room till 18:00 with a phone call. £20
(45,000L) for doubles. Piazza Santo Spirito 9, 50125 Firenze,
tel. 055/215308.

In the same area is **Pensione La Scaletta** (13 Via Guicciardini, tel. 283028, friendly, clean, great rooftop garden, £26 (60,000L) doubles with shower) and **Pensione Adria** (4 Piazza Frescobaldi, tel. 215029, Arno view, £22 (50,000L) doubles).

Also in Oltrarno is the best rock-bottom budget deal in town, the **Ostello Santa Monaca** (6 Via Santa Monaca, a few blocks past Ponte (bridge) Alla Carraia, tel. 268338, over 100 beds for £5 (12,000L) each, large dormitories, well run; no reservations; sign up for available beds during its 9:30-16:00 closed hours. Also very good is the neighbouring **Institute Gould** (49 Via dei Serragli, tel. 212576, smaller, quieter, £17 (40,000L) doubles, office open Mon.-Fri. 9:00-13:00, 15:00-19:00). Farther down Via dei Serragli at No. 106 is **Pensionato Pio X-Artigianelli** (tel. 225044, £6.50 (15,000L) per person), small domitories with showers, open only July, August and September.

There are several good and colourful restaurants in Oltrarno near Piazza Santo Spirito (and Pensione Sorelle Bandini). Try **La Taverna Mescita** (tiny, cheap, good pasta, buffet) at 15 Via dei Michelozzi, **Trattoria Casalinga** (cheap, popular, home cooking) at 9 Via dei Michelozzi or **Trattoria Jerragli** (fun, small, cheap and tasty) two blocks off the piazza at 108 Via dei Serraglia.

Also in Oltrarno is **I Tarocchi**, a great place for pizza or pasta (14 Via dei Renai, tel. 217850, open 19:00-1:00, closed Mondays, meals for £3 (7,000L)).

While there are some special budget restaurants listed in most guidebooks, I generally keep lunch in Florence fast and simple, eating in one of countless self-service places, at a Pizza Rustica or just picnicking (fruit juice, yoghurt, cheese, roll: £2.20 (5,000L)). For an interesting very cheap lunch, try the **Casa di San Francesco** at Piazza S. Annunziata 2 (monastery lunches, noon to 14:30, weekdays, £3.50 (8,000L)). Eat after 14:00 when the museums are closed. Remember, this is Chianti Classico country.

TOUR 11

FLORENCE—ITALIAN HILL TOWNS

Today, finish seeing Florence's sights, then swap big-city bustle for hill-town sleepiness. The hill towns of Tuscany and Umbria offer the visitor a welcome breather from the frantic Venice-Florence-Rome scramble that spells 'Italy' in most itineraries. After the morning in Florence, head south to the ultimate hill town, stranded alone on a pinnacle in a vast canyon—Città di Bagnoregio. Take a big breath and dive into small-town, Old-World Italy.

Suggested Schedule

8:00	Half a day free in Florence. See David, Bargello sculpture museum, shop, gelati.
13:00	Picnic and drive south.
16:00	Arrive at Angelino's.
17:00	Evening walk through Città.
20:00	Dinner in town or at Angelino's. (In the hill towns, be sure you aren't missing any nearby feste.)

Transport

Leave Florence, crossing the St. Nicolo Bridge and following the green signs south by autostrada toward 'Roma'. Drive two hours south to Orvieto, then leave the motorway and wind through fields and farms to Bagnoregio, where the locals (or rusty old signs) will direct you to Angelino Catarcia's Al Boschetto, the only hotel in town.

If you're travelling by train, touring the hill towns is more difficult: Italy's country public transport is miserable. You can take the one-hour bus trip from Orvieto (the nearest station) to Bagnoregio for £1 (2,500L) (3 buses per day) or hitchhike. From Bagnoregio, walk out of town past the gate, turn left at the pyramid monument and right at the first fork to get to the hotel. Without your own wheels it might make sense to use Orvieto as a base: it's a good centre for transport. The tourist office runs several good back-door-style day trips to nearby towns.

Sightseeing Highlights

● ● ●**Città di Bagnoregio**—To reach Città, follow the yellow signs through Bagnoregio. You can drive through the town, or just walk 45 minutes from Angelino's. (If you're driving, look out for the great view of Città from the nearby town of Lubricano.) Park

Civita di Bagnoregio

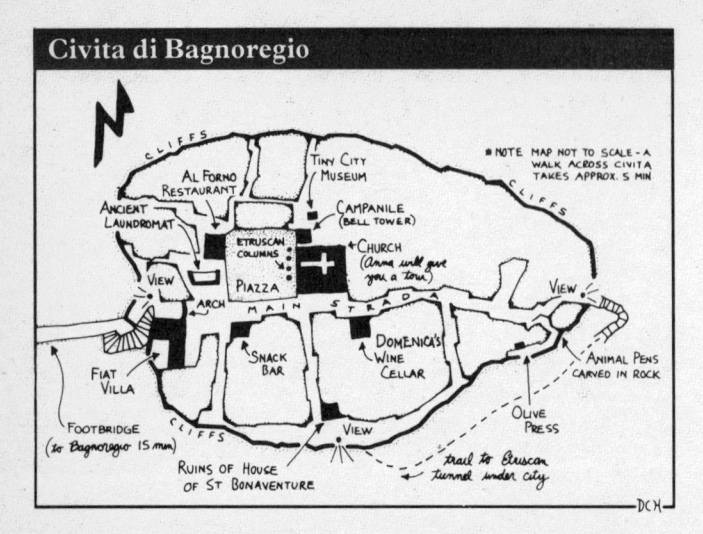

Map labels:
- CLIFFS
- AL FORNO RESTAURANT
- TINY CITY MUSEUM
- ANCIENT LAUNDROMAT
- CAMPANILE (BELL TOWER)
- ETRUSCAN COLUMNS
- CHURCH (Anna will give you a tour)
- PIAZZA
- VIEW
- ARCH
- MAIN STRADA
- VIEW
- FIAT VILLA
- SNACK BAR
- DOMENICA'S WINE CELLAR
- ANIMAL PENS CARVED IN ROCK
- FOOTBRIDGE (to Bagnoregio 15 min)
- VIEW
- OLIVE PRESS
- RUINS OF HOUSE OF ST BONAVENTURE
- trail to Etruscan tunnel under city
- NOTE MAP NOT TO SCALE - A WALK ACROSS CIVITA TAKES APPROX. 5 MIN
- —DCH—

at the far end of Bagnoregio and walk the steep donkey path up to the traffic-free, 2,500-year-old, canyon-swamped pinnacle town of Cività di Bagnoregio. This town is magic, handle it carefully! Al Forno (green door in main square) is the only restaurant in town, and it's great for lunch. Ask for Anna: she'll give a tour of the little church (tip her and buy your postcards from her). Maria runs a nice little museum (ask for 'moo-ZAY-oh') just around the corner. Around the other corner is a cool and friendly wine cellar, where Domenica serves local wine on a dirt floor with stump chairs–350L a glass. Cività offers lots more; it's a treasure hunt.

- **Etruscan Tomb**—Driving from Bagnoregio towards Orvieto, stop just past Purano to tour an Etruscan tomb. Follow the yellow road signs, reading 'Tomba Etrusca', to Giovanni's farm (a sight in itself). If the farmer's home, he'll take you down into the lantern-lit 2,500-year-old tomb discovered 100 years ago by his grandfather. His Italian explanation is fun. Tip him a few thousand lire.
- ● ● **Orvieto**—Umbria's grand hill town is no secret but well worthwhile. Study its colourful Italian Gothic cathedral with exciting Signorelli frescos in the far chapel. Surrounding the striped cathedral are a fine Etruscan museum, a helpful tourist office, a great gelati shop, and unusually clean public toilets. Orvieto is famous for its ceramics and its wine.
- **How about a swim?**—For a fun and refreshing side trip take a dip in Lake Bolsena nestled within an extinct volcano, 30 minutes by car from Bagnoregio. Ristorante Il Faro, below the town of Montefiascone, offers great meals on a leafy terrace overlooking the lake. Good swimming! Nearby in Bomarzo is a monster park (The

Orvieto and Environs

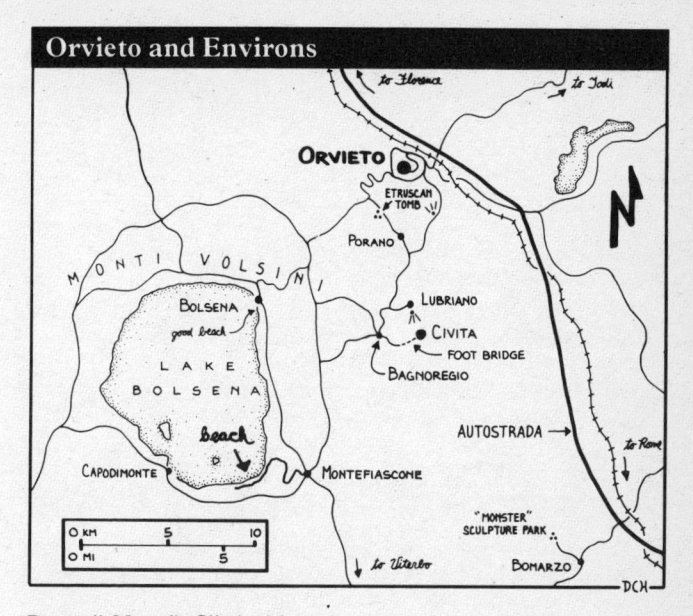

[Map showing Orvieto and surrounding area, including Monti Volsini, Lake Bolsena, Bolsena, Capodimonte, Montefiascone, Bagnoregio, Civita, Lubriano, Porano, Etruscan Tomb, Bomarzo "Monster" Sculpture Park, with roads to Florence, Todi, Rome, and Viterbo.]

Parco di Mostri), filled with stone giants and dragons.

Tuscany—The province just to the north also has some exciting hill towns, many of which are served by trains and more frequent buses. Whatever you do, rip yourself out of the Venice-Florence-Rome syndrome. There's so much more to Italy! Experience the slumber of Umbria and the texture of Tuscany. Seek out and savour uncharted hill towns. For starters, the next map lists a few of my favourites.

Eating and Sleeping

When you leave the tourist crush, life as a traveller in Italy becomes very easy. You should have no trouble finding rooms in the small towns of Italy. You won't even need a list or recommendations.

Just outside Bagnoregio, you'll find Angelino's **Al Boschetto** (£17 (39,000L) per double, bed and breakfast). Angelino doesn't speak English; he doesn't need to. Get an English-speaking Italian to phone him for you from Venice or Florence (tel. 07617/92369. Address: Strada Monterado, Bagnoregio, Viterbo, Italy). His family (Gian Franco, Dominico, Giuseppina and their quintessential Italian grandma) is wonderful and if you so desire, he'll get the boys together and take you deep into the fragrant bowels of the 'Cantina'. Music and vino kill the language barrier in Angelino's wine cellar. Angelino will teach you his theme song,

The hill towns of Tuscany & Umbria

'Trinka, Trinka, Trinka'. The lyrics are easy (see previous sentence). Warning: descend at your own risk—there are no rules unless the female participants set them. If you are lucky enough to eat dinner at Angelino's ('bunny' is the house speciality), ask to try the dolce (sweet) dessert wine. Everything at Angelino's is deliciously homegrown—figs, fruit, wine, rabbit, pasta.

It is possible to find accommodation in private homes in Bagnoregio. Ask for a camera. If you choose to sleep in the bigger 'hill city' of Orvieto, rooms are fairly easy to find there. Visit the tourist office facing the Orvieto cathedral (tel. 0763/41772) to pick up a helpful listing of local hotels.

TOURS 12, 13 & 14

ROME

Rome is magnificent. Your ears will ring, your nose will turn your handkerchief black, you'll be run down or pick-pocketed if you're careless enough, and you'll be frustrated by chaos that only an Italian can understand. But you *must* see Rome. If your hotel provides a comfy refuge; if you pace yourself, accept and even partake in the siesta plan; if you're well-organised for sightseeing; and if you protect yourself and your valuables with extra caution and discretion, you'll do all right. You'll see the sights and leave satisfied. You may even fall in love with the Eternal City.

Suggested Schedule

Tour 12

8:00	Tour Orvieto, Cività, or relax at Angelino's or Lake Bolsena.
11:00	Drive into Rome.
14:00	Find hotel, siesta.
16:00	Walk through ancient Rome: Colosseum, Forum, Capitol Hill.
20:00	Dinner in Campo dei Fioro.

Tour 13

9:00	Pantheon.
10:00	Curious sights near Pantheon.
12:00	Self-service or picnic lunch.
14:00	Siesta, free afternoon. Options: Ostia, E.U.R., Villa Borghese, shopping.
18:00	Taxi to Trastevere for dinner. Walk through Rome at night: Campo dei Fiori, Piazza Navona, Trevi Fountain, Spanish Steps, world's largest McDonalds. Metro home (last train, 23:30).

Tour 14

9:00	Vatican Museum and Sistine Chapel, postal chores.
12:00	Picnic in Via Andrea Doria Market.
14:00	St. Peter's Basilica. Church, crypt, walk to top of dome (allow one hour), treasury, square. Great free English tours normally at 15:15 from portico.
18:00	The '*Dolce Vita* stroll' down the Via del Corso.

Rome wasn't built in a day—nor can it be seen in a day—so I suggest two and a half. Focusing selectively on the highlights of Ancient Rome, baroque Rome and the Vatican, you can accomplish plenty in a short well-organised visit.

Transport: Bagnoregio—Orvieto—Rome

After an easy morning in hill-town Italy, wind back to Orvieto where you hop back on the *autostrada* for the quick one-hour drive to Rome. At the edge-of-Rome service area there's a motorway tourist office. If open, use their great room-finding service, confirm sightseeing plans, buy the cheap Rome book and pick up a city map. Greater Rome is circled by the *Grande Raccordo Anulare*. This ring road has spokes that lead you into the centre. Entering from the north, take the Via Salaria exit and work your way doggedly into the thick of things. Avoid driving in Rome during rush hour. (You may find every hour is rush hour but some are even worse than others.) Drive defensively: Roman cars stay in their lanes like rocks in an avalanche. Parking in Rome is dangerous: choose a well-lit busy street or a safe area. Get advice at your hotel. My favourite hotel is next to the Ministry of Defence—guarded by machine-gunners. In Rome, when all else fails, hire a taxi and follow him to your hotel.

By train things are much easier. The Orvieto-Rome trains are fast and frequent, zipping you straight into the centrally located Roma-Termini station. Use train time to eat, study and plan. Some trains stop only at one of Rome's suburban stations which each have convenient connections to the central 'Termini' station.

Orientation

Rome at its peak meant civilisation itself. Everything was either civilised (part of the Roman Empire), or barbarian (dark, chaotic and without lawyers). Today, Rome is Italy's leading city, the capital of Catholicism and a splendid…'junkpile' is not quite the right word…of Western civilisation. As you wander you'll find its buildings, people, cats, laundry and traffic to be endlessly entertaining. And then, of course, there are its magnificent sights.

You will find it easy to walk in the ancient city. The best of the classical sights stand in a line from the Colosseum to the Pantheon. The medieval city lies between the Pantheon and the river. The night life and high-class shopping twinkle in or near the Via del Corso, Rome's main street. The Vatican City is a compact world of its own, as is the seedy/colourful wrong-side-of-the-river Trastevere area—village Rome at its best. The modern sprawl of Rome, on the other hand, is of no interest to us; our Rome is the old core—basically within the triangle formed by the station, Colosseum, and Vatican.

Roma/Rome

(map of Rome showing landmarks including Vatican City, St. Peters, Vatican Museum, Castello S. Angelo, Villa Borghese, Nat'l Museum, Nat'l Mod. Art Gallery, Borghese Gallery (great Bernini), S. Maria Cncl. (Capuchin crypt-bones), Spanish Steps, Via Veneto, Nat'l Museum of Rome, EPT (buses), Termini Stazione, Main Post Office, Via del Tritone, Piazza Barberini, Trevi Fountain, Nardizzi's, Piazza Navona, Pantheon, Piazza Venezia, S. Maria Maggiore, to Napoli, Firenze, Corso Victor Emanuele, Gianicolo, Campodoglio (museums), V. Emanuele, Forum, S. Pietro in Vincoli (Moses by Michelangelo), Piazza Garibaldi, S. Maria Trastevere (colorful old Rome), Palantino, Colosseum, Tempietto, S. Giovanni in Laterano, Circus Maximus, Baths of Caracalla (out door opera in summer), to E.U.R., to Via Appia Antica. Legend: 1 Convent, 2 Convent, 3 Self Service Rest., 4 Pension Alimandi)

Tourist Information: The *Ente Provinciale Per il Turismo* (EPT) has two offices: the one in the station (very crowded, open daily 9:00-19:00, tel. 465461 or 4750078), and the central office (just a five-minute walk away, off Piazza della Republica, less crowded, similar hours but closed Sundays, tel. 463748) have great city maps, brochures with hotels, museum hours, ideas for young travellers, and so on.

The Termini station has many more services: late hours bank, a day hotel, luggage lockers, the bus station and a metro stop.

Transport in Rome

Never drive in Rome if you can avoid it. This sightseeing plan groups most of your sightseeing into areas so you'll be on foot a lot. Public transport, however, should be used liberally. It's logical, inexpensive, and part of your Roman fertility rite. Taxis are not expensive—if the meter is turned on. Three or four travelling together should taxi almost everywhere. Rather than wave and wave, ask in local shops for the nearest taxi stand. Bus routes are charted on most maps and clearly listed at the stops. Buy tickets at *tabac* shops (punch them yourself on board) and learn why the system is named ATAC.

The Roman metro system (Metropolitan) is very basic, but also very convenient: it's clean, cheap and fast; take advantage of it. While much of Rome is not served by its skimpy two-line metro, these stops may be helpful to you: Termini (central station, National Museum), Barberini (Piccadilly's Restaurant, Cappuccin Crypt, Trevi Fountain), Spagna (Spanish Steps, Villa Borghese, top-class shopping area), Flamino (Piazza del Popolo, start of the Via del Corso *Dolce Vita* stroll), Ottaviano (the Vatican), Colosseo (the Colosseum, Roman Forum) and E.U.R. (Mussolini's futuristic suburb). Save time and legwork whenever possible by telephoning. When the feet are about to give out, sing determinedly, 'I'm a Roman in the gloamin'...'

Sightseeing Highlights

● ● ●**Colosseum**—*The* great example of Roman engineering, 2,000 years old. Putting two theatres together, the Romans created an amphitheatre capable of seating 50,000 people. Read up on it. Climb to the top. Watch out for gypsy thief gangs—usually very young timid-looking girls. Get the small red books with plastic overleafs to unruin the ruins. They're priced at £8.50 (20,000L)—pay only 10,000. Very helpful. Open daily 9:00-19:00, free.

● ● ●**Roman Forum (Foro Romano)**—The civic centre of the city and its birthplace. The common ground of the seven hills, the Forum is frustrating to many visitors. To help resurrect this rubble, study the before-and-after pictures in the cheap city guidebooks sold on the streets. Your basic Forum sights are: Basilica Aemilia (on your right as you walk down the entry ramp, floor plan of this ancient palace shows how medieval churches adopted this basilica design); Via Sacra (main street of ancient Rome running from the Arch of Septimius Severus on right, past Basilica Aemilia, over to Arch of Titus and the Colosseum on left); Basilica Maxentius (giant barrel-vault remains of a huge building looming crumbly and weed-eaten to the left of Via Sacra as you walk to Arch of Titus); and the Palantine Hill (walk up to right from Arch of Titus to the remains of the Imperial palaces, pleasant garden with a good Forum view and, on the far side, a view of the dusty old Circus Maximus). Open 9:00-18:00, Sun. 9:00-13:00, closed Tuesday, £2.20 (5,000L).

●**St. Peter-in-Chains Church (San Pietro in Vincoli)**—On show are the original chains and Michelangelo's Moses in an otherwise unexceptional church. Just a short walk from the Colosseum. 6:30-12:30, 15:00-19:00.

Mammertine Prison—The 2,500-year-old converted cistern which once imprisoned Saints Peter and Paul is worth a look.

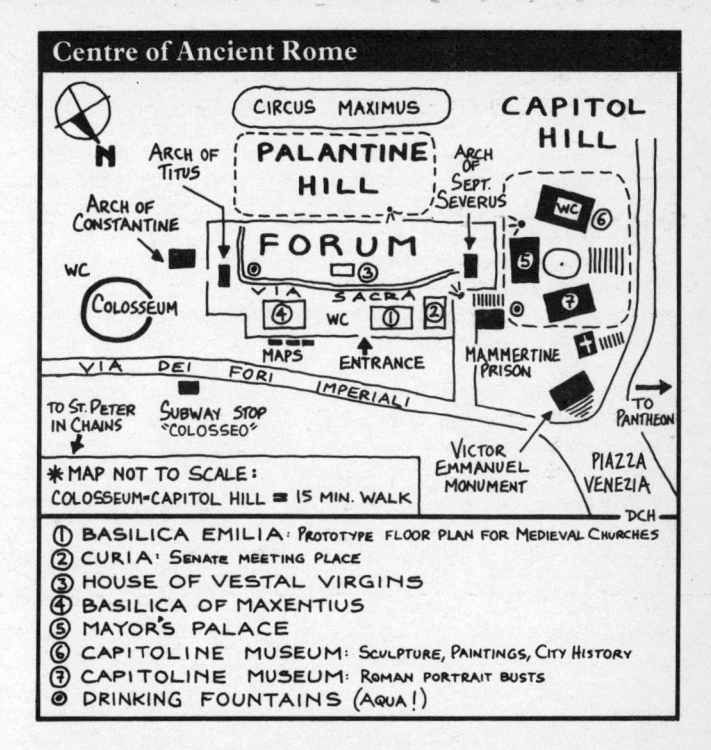

Centre of Ancient Rome

Map showing: Circus Maximus, Palatine Hill, Capitol Hill, Arch of Titus, Arch of Sept. Severus, Arch of Constantine, Colosseum, Forum, Via Sacra, WC, Maps, Entrance, Mammertine Prison, Via dei Fori Imperiali, To St. Peter in Chains, Subway Stop "Colosseo", Victor Emmanuel Monument, Piazza Venezia, To Pantheon.

✳ MAP NOT TO SCALE:
COLOSSEUM=CAPITOL HILL ≈ 15 MIN. WALK

① BASILICA EMILIA: Prototype floor plan for Medieval Churches
② CURIA: Senate meeting place
③ HOUSE OF VESTAL VIRGINS
④ BASILICA OF MAXENTIUS
⑤ MAYOR'S PALACE
⑥ CAPITOLINE MUSEUM: Sculpture, Paintings, City History
⑦ CAPITOLINE MUSEUM: Roman portrait busts
⊙ DRINKING FOUNTAINS (AQUA!)

On the walls are lists of prisoners (Christian and non-Christian) and how they were executed (*Strangolati, Morto di Fame*, etc.). At the top of the stairs leading to the Campidoglio you'll find a refreshing water fountain. Block the spout with your fingers—it spurts up for drinking. Open 9:00-12:30, 14:00-18:30.

• **Capitoline Hill (Campidoglio)**—This hill was the religious and political centre of ancient Rome and has been the home of the civic government for 800 years. Michelangelo's lovely square is bounded by two fine museums and the mayoral palace. The Capitoline Museum in the Palazzo Nuovo (the building closest to the river) is the world's oldest museum (500 years old) and more important than its sister (opposite). Outside the entrance, notice the marriage announcements. You may see a few blissfully attired newlyweds as well. Inside the courtyard have some photo fun with chunks of a giant statue of Emperor Constantine. (A rare public toilet hides near the museum ticket taker.) The museum is worthwhile, with lavish rooms housing several great statues including the original (500 B.C.) Etruscan Capitoline wolf and the enchanting Commodus as Hercules. Across the square is a museum

full of ancient statues—great if you like portrait busts of forgotten
emperors. (Both open Tues.-Sat. 9:00-14:00, Tues. and Thurs.
17:00-20:00, Sat. 20:30-23:00, Sun. 9:00-13:00.)

Don't miss the great view of the Forum from the terrace just
past the mayor's palace on the right. Walk halfway down the
grand stairway toward Piazza Venezia. From here, walk back up to
approach the great square the way Michelangelo wanted you to.
At the bottom of the stairs, look up the long stairway to your right
for a good example of the earliest style of Christian church—and
be thankful you don't need to climb these steps. Down the street
on your left you'll see a modern building actually built around
surviving ancient pillars and arches. Farther ahead, look into the
ditch (on the right) and see how everywhere modern Rome is built
upon the countless bricks and forgotten mosaics of ancient Rome.
Piazza Venezia—This square is the focal point of modern Rome.
The Via del Corso, starting here, is the city's axis (surrounded by
the best shopping district). From the Palazzo di Venezia's balcony
above the square, Mussolini whipped up the nationalistic fervour of
Italy, and the Fascist masses filled the square screaming, 'Il Duce!'
(Fifteen years later they hung him from a meat hook in Milan).
Victor Emmanuel Monument—Loved only by the ignorant and
his relatives, most Romans call this oversize memorial to the
Italian king 'the wedding cake', 'the typewriter' or 'the dentures'. It
wouldn't be so bad if it weren't sitting on a priceless acre of ancient
Rome. The soldiers there guard Italy's Tomb of the Unknown
Soldier.

● ● ●**Pantheon**—For the greatest look at the splendour of Rome,
this best-preserved interior of antiquity is a must (open 9:00-14:00,
possibly later, Sun. 9:00-13:00, closed Monday). Walk past its
one-piece marble columns and through its original bronze door. Sit
inside under the glorious skylight and study it. The dome, 140
feet high and wide, was Europe's largest until Brunelleschi's dome
was built in Florence 1,200 years later. You'll understand why
this wonderfully harmonious architecture was so inspirational to the
artists of the Renaissance, particularly Raphael who, along with
Italy's first two kings, chose to be buried here. As you leave notice
the 'rise of Rome'...about 10 feet since the Pantheon was built.
This is the only continously used building of ancient Rome.

● ●**Curiosities near the Pantheon**—In a little square behind
the Pantheon to the left, past the Bernini elephant and Egyptian
obelisk statue, is Santa Maria sopra Minerva, Rome's only Gothic
church (built over a pre-Christian Temple of Minerva) with a
little-known Michelangelo statue, Christ Bearing the Cross. Nearby
(leave by the church's rear door behind the Michelangelo statue and
turn left) you'll find the church, Chiesa di Ignazio, with a fake (and
flat) cupola. Just past the busy street a few blocks south is the very

rich and baroque Gesù Church, headquarters of the Jesuits.
● ●**Piazza Navona**—Rome's most interesting night scene features street music, artists, fire eaters, local Casanovas, great chocolate ice cream (*tartufo*, best at Tre Scalini), outdoor cafes, hippies, and three Bernini fountains (he's the father of baroque art); this oblong square is moulded around the long-gone stadium of Domitian, an ancient chariot race track. The nearby Campo dei Fiori offers a colourful produce and flower market by day, and a romantic outdoor dining room after dark.
●**The 'Dolce Vita stroll' down Via del Corso**—The city's chic 'cruise' here from the Piazza del Popolo down a wonderfully traffic-free section of the Via del Corso each evening around 18:00. You can study high fashion, antiques, and humanity. Shoppers, turn left for the Spanish Steps and Gucci. Historians, continue down the Via del Corso to the Victor Emmanuel Monument, climb Michaelangelo's stairway to his glorious Campidoglio Square and visit Rome's open-in-the-evening (Tues., Thurs. and Sat.) Capitoline museum. Catch the lovely view of the Forum (past mayor's palace on right) as the horizon reddens.
●**Villa Borghese**—Rome's 'Hyde Park' is great for people-watching (plenty of modern Romeos and Juliets). You can row on the lake, and visit its three museums featuring Baroque paintings, an Etruscan collection and modern art.
●**National Museum of Rome (Museo Nazionale Romano delle Terme)**—Directly in front of the station, it houses much of the greatest ancient Roman sculpture. Open 9:00-14:00, Sun. until 13:00, closed Monday £1.75 (4,000L).
●**Trastevere**—The best look at old modern Rome is across the Tiber River. Witness colourful street scenes: pasta rollers, street-wise cats, crinkly old political posters encrusting graffiti-laden walls. There are motionless men in sleeveless T-shirts framed by open windows, cobbles with centuries of life ground into their cleavages, kids kicking footballs into the cars that litter their alley-fields. The action all marches to the chime of the church bells. Go there and wander. Wonder. Be a poet. This is Rome's 'Left Bank'. Santa Maria in Trastevere (from the third century) is one of Rome's oldest churches. Notice the ancient basilica floor plan and early Christian symbols in the walls around the entry.
● ●**Ostia Antica**—Rome's ancient seaport (100,000 people in the time of Caesar, later a ghost town, now excavated) is the next best thing to Pompeii and, I think, Europe's most under-rated sight. Start at the 2,000-year-old theatre, buy a map, and explore the town, finishing with its marvellous little museum. Get there by taking the metro to the 'Piramide' stop and catching the 'Lido' train to Ostia (twice an hour, 40p (1,000L)). Walk over the overpass

Vatican City, St. Peter's & the Museum

Map features:
- Ottaviano Subway Stop
- Via Andrea Doria
- Via Ottaviano
- Via Leone
- Convent
- Market
- Pensione Alimandi
- Piazza di Risorgimento (Bus Terminal)
- To Tiber River, Pantheoin, Forum etc
- Vatican Museum
- Papal Apt.
- Sistine Chapel
- Gardens
- Radio Vat.
- St. Peter's
- P.O.
- Via della Conciliazione
- Piazza S. Pietro
- Tunnel
- ① Entrance to Vat. Museums
- ② Tourist Info & W.C.

— DCH —

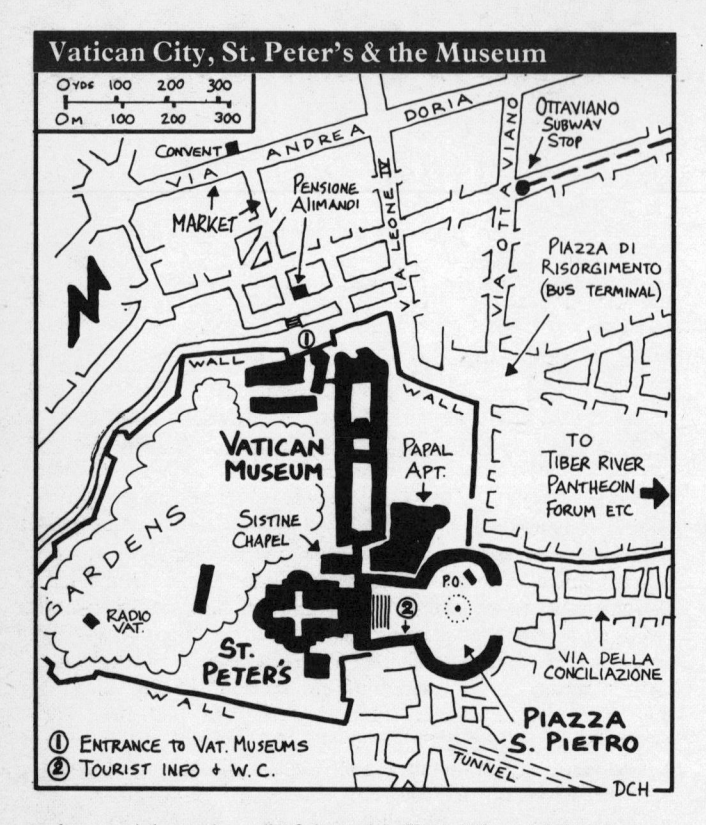

and go straight to the end of that road. Turn left and follow the signs to Ostia Antica. Open daily except Monday from 9:00 to one hour before sunset. The £1.75 (4,000L) entrance fee includes the museum (which closes at 13:00). Just beyond is the beach (Lido)—interesting, but crowded and filthy.

The Vatican City—This tiny independent country of just over 100 acres is contained entirely within Rome. Politically powerful, the Vatican is the religious capital of 800 million Roman Catholics: it deserves maximum respect regardless of your religious beliefs. Start your visit by calling at the helpful tourist office just to the left of St. Peter's Basilica (tel. 6984466; pick up a map of the country and of the church, ask about tours). Open Mon.-Sat., 8:30-18:30. Telephone them if you're interested in their almost-daily morning tours of the Vatican grounds. Also, if you plan to take the afternoon English tour of the church, phone to confirm the time (usually around 15:00).

St. Peter's Basilica

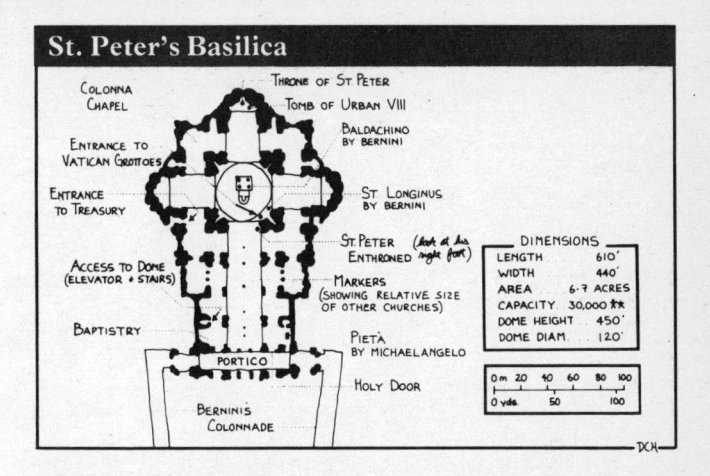

Floor plan labels:
- COLONNA CHAPEL
- THRONE OF ST PETER
- TOMB OF URBAN VIII
- BALDACHINO BY BERNINI
- ENTRANCE TO VATICAN GROTTOES
- ENTRANCE TO TREASURY
- ST LONGINUS BY BERNINI
- ST PETER (look at his right foot) ENTHRONED
- ACCESS TO DOME (ELEVATOR + STAIRS)
- MARKERS (SHOWING RELATIVE SIZE OF OTHER CHURCHES)
- BAPTISTRY
- PIETÀ BY MICHAELANGELO
- PORTICO
- HOLY DOOR
- BERNINI'S COLONNADE

DIMENSIONS
- LENGTH 610'
- WIDTH 440'
- AREA 6.7 ACRES
- CAPACITY 30,000
- DOME HEIGHT 450'
- DOME DIAM. 120'

●●● **St. Peter's Basilica**—There is no doubt: this is the biggest, richest and most impressive church on earth. To call it vast is an understatement: marks on the floor show where the next largest churches would fit if they were put inside; the ornamental cherubs would dwarf a large man. Birds roost inside, and thousands of people wander about, heads craned heavenward, hardly noticing each other. Don't miss Michelangelo's Pietà (behind bullet-proof glass) to the right of the entrance. Bernini's altar work and huge bronze canopy (the *baldachino*) are brilliant. The treasury and the crypt are also important (open 9:00-18:30). Wonderful English guided tours (free, 90 minutes) normally leave at 15:15 from the portico. A guide or guidebook is essential.

The dome, Michelangelo's last work, is (of course) the biggest anywhere. Taller than a football field is long, it's well worth the climb (537 steps, allow an hour to go up and down) for a great view of Rome, the Vatican grounds and the inside of the Basilica (open 8:00-18:00 daily, closing at 17:00 out of season, last entry is about an hour before closing. Catch the lift inside the church). The church strictly enforces its dress code. Dress modestly—a dress or long trousers, shoulders covered. St. Peter's is open daily from 7:00 to 19:00.

●●● **The Vatican Museum**—Too often, the immense Vatican Museum is treated as an obstacle course separating the tourist from the Sistine Chapel. Even without the Sistine, this is one of Europe's top three or four houses of art. It can be exhausting, so plan your visit carefully, focusing on a few themes, and allow several hours. (Required: Sistine Chapel and Raphael Rooms, the classical statuary of the Pio-Clementine collection, and the Pinacoteca painting collection with Raphael's Transfiguration.

Recommended: Modern religious art, Egyptain, Etruscan.) The
museum clearly marks out four colour-coded visits of different
lengths. Headphones (£2.20 (5,000L)) give a recorded tour of
the Raphael rooms and Michelangelo's Sistine masterpiece. These
rooms are the pictorial culmination of the Renaissance. (Summer
hours: 9:00-17:00, Sat. 9:00-14:00; out of season: 9:00-14:00.) Last
entry an hour before closing. Many minor rooms close from 13:45
to 14:45 or from 13:30 on. £3 (7,000L).

The museum book-and-card shop is great, offering, for example, a
priceless (£4.50 (10,000L)) black-and-white photo book of the Pietà,
which I stock up on for gifts. The museum (and the Piazza San
Pietro) has a Vatican post office with comfortable writing rooms;
the Vatican post is the only reliable postal service in Italy, and the
stamps are a collectible bonus.

• **Cappuccin Crypt**—If you want bones, this is it: below Santa
Maria della Concezione in Via Veneto, just off Piazza Barberini, are
thousands of skeletons, all artistically arranged for the delight—
or disgust—of the always wide-eyed visitor. Read the monastic
message on the wall near the entrance so you'll understand this is
more than just an exercise in bony gore. Pick up a few of Rome's
most interesting postcards. (Open 9:00-12:00, 15:00-18:30. Bank
with long hours and good exchange rates next door.)

• **E.U.R.**—Mussolini's planned suburb of the future (50 years
ago) is just a ten-minute metro ride (to E.U.R.-Marconi) from the
Colosseum. Very impressive Fascist architecture, with a history
museum including a large-scale model of ancient Rome.

Overrated Sights—The Spanish Steps (with the world's largest
McDonalds—McGrandeur at its best—just down the street)
and Trevi Fountaini (but very central, free and easy to see,
best at night) are famous only because they are famous. The
commercialized catacombs, which contain no bones, are way out of
the city and not worth the time or trouble.

Entertainment

Night time fun in Rome is found in the piazzas, along the river,
and at its outdoor concerts and street fairs. Pick up the local
periodical entertainment guide *Qui Roma* (Here's Rome) or the
English monthly misnamed *This Week in Rome* for a rundown on
special events.

A highlight for many is a grand and lavish opera performance
on the world's biggest opera stage, the ruins of the ancient Baths
of Caracalla (*Terme di Caracalla*). (Tickets £6.50 (15,000L) and
up; shows start at 21:00 several nights a week throughout July and
August; English scripts available, tel. 461755.)

The social whirlpools make the famous floodlit nightspots
(Navona, Trevi, Espagna, Corso) endlessly entertaining. Sit in a
cafe and watch the world stay young. La dolce vitamin!

Helpful Hints
In museums, 'A.C.' (*Avanti Christo*, or 'Before Christ') after a year is the same as our B.C. 'D.C.' (*Dopo Christo*) is what we call A.D. Shops and offices are open 9:00-13:00, 16:00-20:00; museums, 9:00-14:00. Most museums close on Mondays (except the Vatican) and at 13:00 on Sundays. Outdoor sights like the Colosseum, Forum and Ostia Antica are open 9:00-19:00 (or one hour before sunset), often closed one day a week. The Capitoline Hill museums are Rome's only nocturnal museums, open Tuesdays and Thursdays, 17:00-20:00 and Saturdays 20:30-23:00. Churches open very early, close for lunch and reopen for a few hours around 16:00. Dress modestly—no bare shoulders or shorts.

Eating and Sleeping
Rome is difficult only because of its overwhelming size. There are plenty of rather tatty pensions, *locande*, and *alberghi* offering budget (£6 (14,000L) per person) beds around the station. Via Palestro, Via Castelfidardo, and Via Principe Amadeo, all near the station, have dozens of cheap places.

The convents of the city are your most interesting budget bet. The *Protezione delle Giovane* (in the station, erratic hours, tel. 4751594) is a helpful—mostly to women—convent and budget room-finding service. Convents operate tax-free, so are cheaper; these are obviously peaceful, safe and clean, but sometimes stern, and usually 'no speak English'. Try the **Suore di Sant' Anna** (single rooms—£5.70 (13,000L), breakfast—£1.75 (4,000L), lunch or dinner—great £4.50 (10,000L) value, at Piazza Madonna dei Monti 3, 00184 Roma, tel. 06/485778, three blocks from the Forum at Via Serpentine and Via Baccina); it was built for Ukrainian pilgrims—not a privileged class in the U.S.S.R.—and is therefore rarely full (although it's crowded with groups in June and September). The sisters speak Italian, Portuguese and, of course, Ukrainian—Good luck! If you land a spot, your blessings will include great atmosphere, heavenly meals, unbeatable location—and a rock-bottom price.

Near the Vatican Museum at 42 Via Andrea Doria (buzz the big grey gate) is the **Suore Oblate Dell' Assunzione** convent (tel. 3599540, £6 (14,000L) per night, no meals). Spanish, French and Italian spoken in an interesting area across from a colourful market. Just across the street from the Vatican Museum is the **Convent** at Viale Vaticano 92 (£6 (14,000L) per person, tel. 350209). They take men and women but no reservations, and are normally full but worth a try.

In Rome, I usually splash out on a nicer hotel, providing an oasis/refuge that makes it easier to enjoy this intense and grinding city. My choices for more normal accommodation are

Pensione Alimandi (friendly, speaks English, £20 (46,000L) doubles with breakfast, great roof garden; one block in front of the Vatican Museum, Via Tunisi 8, 00192 Roma, tel. 06/6799343) and **Pensione Nardizzi** (Via Firenze 38, 00184 Roma, tel. 06/460368, in a safe handy and central location, five-minute walk from central station and Piazza Barberini on the corner of Via Firenze and Via XX Septembre.); Pension Nardizzi is expensive (£25-£30 (60,000-72,000L) per double with breakfast) but worth the money. Sr. Nardizzi speaks English and stocks great free Rome maps.

The cheapest meals in town are picnics (from *alimentari* shops or open-air markets) and stand-up or take-away meals from a **Pizza Rustica** (pizza sold by the weight). The best restaurants seem to be on the smallest streets off main thoroughfares.

Hotels can recommend the best nearby cafeteria or restaurant. A handy self-service cafeteria is **Il Delfino**, corner of Via Argentina and Via Vittorio Emmanuel near the Pantheon. Classier and also near the Pantheon (two blocks in front down Via Maddalena, around the corner to the left, ask for directions at the paper shop in Pantheon Square) is **Hostaria La Nuova Capannina**, at Piazza della Coppelle 8, close to Pantheon, with good, moderately priced sit-down meals. If your convent serves food, sup thee there. In Trastevere, I enjoy **Il Comparone** at Piazza in Piscinula 47, tel. 5816249. Near the Piazza Navona, try the restaurants in **Campo dei Fiori** for good food and great atmosphere. **Piccadilly's** in Piazza Barberini is good value, and the nearby **Ristorante Il Giardino** (Via Zucchelli 29, tel 465202, closed Mondays) is my favourite spot for splashing out.

Near the Vatican Museum and Pension Alimandi, try **Ristorante dei Musei** (corner of Via Sebastiano Veneiro and Via Santamaura) or one of several good places along Via Sebastiano Veneiro. **Trattoria dei Turisti**, on Via Leone IV, **La Rustichella da Carlo**, at Via Angelo Emo 1, and the **Rosticceria** at the corner of Via Vespasiano and Viale Giulio Cesare (cheap, easy and has pleasant outdoor seating), are all good. Don't miss the wonderful Via Andrea Doria market at the bottom of the steps (closed by 13:00).

TOUR 15

NORTH TO PISA—ITALIAN RIVIERA

Leave Rome early and speed to Pisa for lunch and a chance to scale that leaning tower. Then it's on to the sunny and remote chunk of the Italian Riviera called the Cinque Terre where you'll stay for two nights. This is a much-needed break after the intensity of Venice, Florence and Rome. You couldn't see a museum here if you wanted to—just sun, sea, sand, wine, and pure unadulterated Italy.

Suggested Schedule

8:00	Drive north to Pisa.
13:00	Picnic lunch, climb tower, sightsee in Pisa.
15:00	Drive to La Spezia.
16:30	Train to Cinque Terre.
Evening	Free time in Vernazza.

Transport

With breakfast and plenty of cappuccino under your belt, hit the *autostrada* and drive north for about five hours, turning left at Florence, stopping at Pisa for lunch. You might consider beating the traffic by leaving before breakfast. The quickest way out of Rome, regardless of which way you're heading, is the shortest way to the ring road (*Raccordo*).

Pisa, a 30-minute drive out of the way, can be seen in about an hour. Its three important sights float regally on a lush lawn—the best grass in Italy, ideal for a picnic. The 'Piazza of Miracles' is the home of the famous Leaning Tower. The climb to the top is fun (294 tilted steps, open 8:00-19:30). The huge cathedral (open 7:45-12:45, 15:00-18:45) is actually more important artistically than its more famous tipsy bell tower. Finally, the Baptistry (same hours as church) is interesting for its great acoustics; if you ask nicely and leave a tip, the doorman uses its echo-power to sing haunting harmonies with himself. Pisa has plenty of hotels, and you could make it your base for a side trip into the Cinque Terre by direct train.

One hour north is the port of La Spezia, where you'll park your car (hopefully at the station; otherwise, find a safe spot) and catch the 600-lire, 20-minute train into the Cinque Terre, Italy's Riviera wonderland.

Cinque Terre Train Schedule
Trains leaving La Spezia for the Cinque Terre villages:
1:10, 4:02, 4:50, 5:36, 6:42, 7:40, 9:05, 10:30, 11:39, 12:22, 13:25, 14:33, 15:27, 17:06, 17:52, 18:10, 19:08, 19:45, 21:20, 22:40, 23:40.
Trains leaving Vernazza for La Spezia: 0:32, 1:30, 4:40, 5:13, 5:49, 6:09, 6:56, 7:16, 8:39, 9:49, 10:55, 11:03, 12:17, 13:30, 14:37, 15:49, 16:50, 17:30, 18:42, 19:05, 19:34, 20:35, 22:01, 22:42.

The trains listed above stop at each Cinque Terre town. On the map, towns 1, 2, 3 and 5 are just a few minutes before or after Vernazza, town 4. These trains are in the *Locale* class (Italian for 'milk train'). Trains often run late.

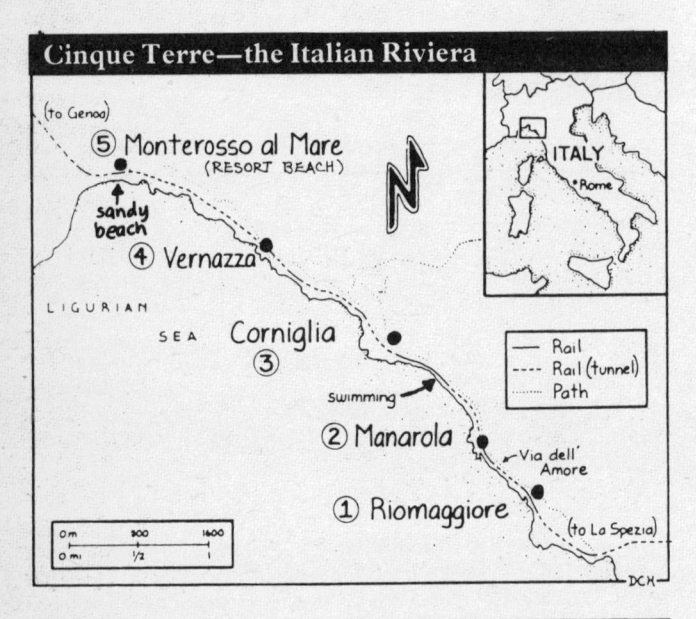

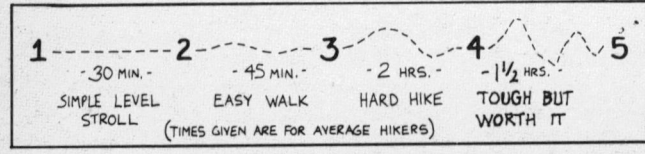

Cinque Terre—the Italian Riviera

(to Genoa)
⑤ Monterosso al Mare (RESORT BEACH)
sandy beach
④ Vernazza
LIGURIAN SEA
Corniglia ③
swimming
② Manarola
Via dell' Amore
① Riomaggiore
(to La Spezia)

ITALY • Rome

— Rail
--- Rail (tunnel)
····· Path

```
1 --------- 2 --------- 3 --------- 4 --------- 5
   -30 MIN.-    -45 MIN.-    -2 HRS.-   -1½ HRS.-
  SIMPLE LEVEL  EASY WALK   HARD HIKE  TOUGH BUT
    STROLL  (TIMES GIVEN ARE FOR AVERAGE HIKERS) WORTH IT
```

This chart shows walking time between the five villages of the Cinque Terre, as numbered on the map above. (Thinking of towns as numbers simplifies your beach life.)

Orientation

Vernazza, one of the five towns in the region, is the ideal base, where, if you've phoned in advance, Sr. Sorriso will have dinner waiting. In the evening, wander down the main street (also the only street) to the harbour to join the visiting Italians in a sing-along. Have a *gelato*, cappuccino or glass of the local Cinque Terre wine at a waterfront cafe or on the bar's patio that overlooks the breakwater (follow the rope railing above the football field, notice the photo of rough seas just above the door inside). Stay up as late as you like because tomorrow is your holiday from your holiday—nothing scheduled!

Eating and Sleeping

While the Cinque Terre is unknown to the international mobs that ravage the Spanish and French coasts, plenty of Italians come here, so getting a room can be tough. August and weekends are bad. At weekends in August, forget it! But the area is worth planning ahead for.

In Vernazza, my favourite town, stay at **Pensione Sorriso** (it's the only place in town, and Sr. Sorriso knows it), up the street from the station (£20 (44,000L)) per person includes bed, breakfast, dinner, a Mediterranean-style toilet in the bar and the catchiest video game tune you'll ever have no choice but to like, 19018 Vernazza, Cinque Terre, La Spezia, tel. 0187/812224, English spoken). If that's full or too expensive, Sr. Sorriso will help you find a private room (£8.50 (20,000L) per person). You can ask around yourself at the local bars and save a little money. (For a £30 (70,000L) fine, you can sleep free on the beach.)

In Riomaggiore, **Hotel Argentina** is above the town at Via di Gasperi 37 (tel. 0187/920213, £17 (40,000L) doubles, £20 (46,000L) triples, run by friendly Andrea and Irene Vivaldi). The local tobacco shop has a listing of all the private rooms in town, and the restaurant in the centre of town can usually find you a room in a private home (*camera*) for £6 (14,000L). Riomaggiore also has a new informal **youth hostel**, one block inland from the station at Via Signorini 41, where Rosa Ricci offers cooking facilities, a bed and shower for £4.50 (10,000L). No English, tel. 0187/92050.

In Manarola, **Marina Piccola** is located right on the water (tel. 0187/920103, around £27 (60,000L) per double).

Many enjoy staying in Monterosso al Mare, the most beach-resorty of the five Cinque Terre towns. There are plenty of hotels, beach umbrellas for hire, and cars. Nearby Lerici is a pleasant town with several reasonable harbour-side hotels and a daily boat connection to Vernazza. Boat in, train home. When all else fails, you can stay in a noisy bigger town like La Spezia and take side trips into the villages.

Sorriso requires that you take dinner from his pension; it's a forced luxury, and there is often fresh seafood; his house wine is great. If you have an excuse to really celebrate, have his strong, subtly sweet and unforgettable Sciachetra (shock-ee-tra) wine.

Elsewhere in Vernazza, the expensive **Castello** (castle) restaurant serves great food just under the castle with Vernazza twinkling below you and friendly Lorenzo at your service. The town's only *gelati* shop is excellent, and most harbour-side bars will let you take your glass on a breakwater stroll. The pizza bar on the main street serves a fantastic blend of crust, sauce, cheese and spice—by the slice.

TOUR 16

HOLIDAY FROM YOUR HOLIDAY: THE ITALIAN RIVIERA

Take a free day to enjoy the villages, swimming, walking, sunshine, wine and evening romance of one of God's great gifts to tourism. Pay attention to the schedules, and take advantage of the trains.

Helpful Hints

Pack your beach and swimming gear, wear your walking shoes and catch the train to Riomaggiore. Walk along the cliff-hanging Via dell' Amore to Manarola and buy food for a picnic, then walk to Corniglia for a rocky but pleasant beach. There's a shower there, a bar, and a cafe that serves light food. The swimming is great and there's a train to zip you home later on. Or walk on to Vernazza where you can enjoy the sweet sounds of the village's asylum for crazed roosters who cock-a-doodle at any hour—except dawn.

If you're into *il dolce far niente* and don't want to walk, you could take the train directly to Corniglia to maximise beach time.

If you're a walker, walk from Riomaggiore all the way to Monterosso al Mare, where a sandy 'front-door' style beach awaits. Pick a cactus fruit and ask a local to teach you how to peel it, *Delizioso!*

Each beach has showers that probably work better than your hotel's. (Bring soap and shampoo.) Wash clothes today (when you get to Switzerland, your laundry won't dry as fast).

On your last night in Italy, be romantic. Sit on the breakwater, wine in hand, music in the background, and let the warm waves lap at your feet.

Optional Itinerary

Hurried train travellers can take the train overnight to La Spezia from Rome (midnight to 5:30), leave their luggage there, have 14 hours of fun in the Cinque Terre sun. (Walk from Riomaggiore to Monterosso in the cool morning hours, midday on the beaches of towns 5 and 3, dinner and evening in Vernazza.) Then travel overnight again up to Switzerland (Genoa-Luzern 23:25-4:48, scenic Luzern-Interlaken 6:05-8:19); this would overcome the tricky hotel situation altogether. I haven't found anything nearly as nice as the Cinque Terre in this area, so day tripping from this region makes no sense at all.

TOUR 17

FROM THE ITALIAN RIVIERA TO THE ALPS

Today's long drive takes you from palm trees to snowballs: scenic along the Mediterranean coast, boring during the stretch from Genoa to Milan, and thrilling through the Alps. By sunset you'll be nestled down in the very heart of the Swiss Alps—a cathedral even more glorious than St. Peter's.

Suggested Schedule

7:00	Catch train back to your car.
7:30	Take motorway north to Switzerland.
12:30	Lunch in Bellinzona or nearby town.
13:30	Drive to Sustenpass, take a snowball-and-hot-chocolate break.
15:40	Drive to Interlaken, one-hour stop for banking, tourist information and shopping, then on to Stechelberg.
18:45	Catch 18:55 cable car to Gimmelwald.
19:00	Learn why they say, 'If heaven isn't what it's cracked up to be, send me back to Gimmelwald.'

Transport

Catch the 7:00 train (skip Sorriso's breakfast; you'll hurt no one's feelings). If your car's where you left it, drive it on the *autostrada* along the stunning Riviera (expensive tolls because of the many bridges and tunnels). Skirt Christopher Columbus's home town of Genoa, noticing the crowded tower-block living conditions of the Italy that most tourists choose to avoid. Turn north through Italy's industrial heartland, past Milan with its hazy black halo, and on into Switzerland. This is Amaretto country: very cheap at any stop. Just over the border is the Italian-speaking 'Swiss Riviera' with famous resorts like Lugano and Locarno.

Bellinzona is a good town for a lunch break (great picnic area a few miles south of Bellinzona, turn right off the motorway) before climbing to the Alps. After driving through the Italian-speaking Swiss canton of Ticino—famous for its ability to build just about anything out of stone—you'll take the longest tunnel in the world: the ten-mile-long Gotthard Pass Tunnel. It's so boring it's exciting. It hypnotises most passengers into an open-jawed slumber until they pop out into the bright and happy, green and rugged German-speaking Alpine world.

At Wassen (a good place to change money and, according to railway buffs, the best place in Europe for train-watching) turn onto the Sustenpass road (closed in winter, but detouring around to the north is no problem). Higher and higher you'll wind until you're at the snow-bound summit—a good place for a coffee or hot chocolate stop. Give your intended hotel a call, toss a few snowballs, pop in your '*Sound of Music*' cassette and roll on.

Descend into the Bernese Oberland, rounding idyllic Lake Brienz to Interlaken. Stop for an hour there (park at the West Station) to take care of some administrative business. Banks abound; the one in the station is fair and stays open Monday to Saturday until 19:00. A great tourist information office is just past the handy post office on the main street. Interlaken was the first high-class Alpine resort: many of the old elegant hotels along the main street were built in the age of Romanticism (1800s) when for the first time mountains attracted people—and many were climbed...because they were there.

From Interlaken drive 30 minutes south into Lauterbrunnen Valley, a glacier-cut cradle of Swiss-ness. Park at the head of the valley in the Stechelberg car-park (safe and free). Take the huge cable car straight up for five minutes (£2.40 (6 SF)) to traffic-free Gimmelwald village. (Note: Families get a discount on Swiss Alpine lifts. Ask for the family card at any station.) A steep 100-yard climb uphill brings you to the chalet marked simply 'Hotel'. This is Walter Mittler's Hotel Mittaghorn. You have arrived.

For train travellers, the Eurailpass won't work on the mountain lines south of Interlaken. Upon arrival in Interlaken ask about the Jungfrau region trains—schedules, prices and special deals. Also, lay the groundwork for your departure by getting the Interlaken-Bern-Basel-Colmar schedule. The train journey from Interlaken is easy.

Itinerary Options

From the Cinque Terre you could swap Switzerland for France and spend a day in Nice, Cannes and Monte Carlo. Take the night train from Nice to Chamonix via Aix-les-Bains for the best of the French Alps (Mont-Blanc) and take the night-train (20:58-6:42) directly into Paris from there. This plan is much better by train than by car.

Switzerland

- 16,000 square miles.
- 6½ million people (400 per square mile, declining slightly).

■ Switzerland, Europe's richest, best-organised and most mountainous country, is an easy oasis and a breath of fresh Alpine air—much needed after intense Italy.

■ Not unlike the Boy Scouts, the Swiss count cleanliness, neatness, punctuality, independence, thrift and hard work as virtues. They love the awesome nature that surrounds them and are proud of their many achievements. The Swiss standard of living (among the highest in the world), its great social security system and their super-strong currency—not to mention the Alps—give them plenty to be thankful for.

■ Switzerland, 60 per cent of which is rugged Alps has distinct cultural regions and customs. Two-thirds of the people speak German, 20 per cent French, 10 per cent Italian, and a small group of people in the south east speak Romansh, a direct descendant of ancient Latin. Within these four language groups there are many dialects: an interest in these regional distinctions will win the hearts of Swiss you meet. As you travel from one valley to the next, notice changes in architecture and customs.

■ Historically, Switzerland is one of the oldest democracies. Born when three states (cantons) united in 1291, the *Confederatio Helvetica* as it's called (Latin name for the Swiss Federation—notice 'CH' on cars) grew to the 23 of today. The government is very decentralised and the canton is first on the Swiss citizen's list of loyalties.

■ Switzerland loves its neutrality and stayed out of both world wars, but its defences are far from lax: every fit man serves in the army and stays in the reserve; each house has a gun and a bomb shelter; airstrips hide inside mountains behind Batmobile doors; with the push of a button, all road, rail and bridge entrances to the country can be destroyed, changing Switzerland into a formidable mountain fortress. (As you drive, notice the explosive patches on strategic stretches of road.) August 1 is the very festive Swiss national holiday.

■ Swiss Money: The Swiss Franc (SF or F) is divided into 100 rappen (rp) or centimes (c). 1 SF = about 40p and a pound is worth about 2.50 SF. Notice that only the higher denomination coins have ridges.

■ Switzerland has a low inflation rate and a very strong franc. Accommodation, petrol and groceries are reasonable, and walking is free, but alpine lifts and souvenirs are expensive. Shops throughout the land thrill tourists with carved, woven and clanging mountain knick-knacks, clocks, watches, and Swiss Army knives. (Victorinox is the best brand.)

■ The Swiss eat when we do and enjoy rather straightforward, no-nonsense cuisine, delicious fondue, *râclette*, rich chocolates, fresh dairy products (try muesli yogurt), Fendant—a surprisingly good

local white wine—and Rivella, a strange soft drink with milk in it.
The Co-op and Migros grocers are the hungry hiker's best budget
bet.

■ You can get anywhere quickly on Switzerland's superb road
system (the world's most expensive to build per mile: you drivers
will have no choice but to help out by buying the £15
(35 SF) annual Swiss motorway permit at the border) or on its
scenic and efficient trains. Tourist information offices abound.
While Switzerland's booming big cities are quite cosmopolitan, the
traditional culture lives on in the Alpine villages: spend most of
your time getting high in the Alps. On Sundays you're most likely
to enjoy traditional sports, music, clothing and culture.

Eating and Sleeping

While Switzerland bustles, Gimmelwald sleeps. It has a youth
hostel, a pension, and a hotel. The **hostel** is simple, less than clean,
rowdy, cheap (£2.40 (6 SF)) and very friendly. It's often full,
so phone ahead to Lena, the elderly woman who runs the place (tel.
036/55.17.04). It has a self-serve kitchen and is one block from the
cable car station. This relaxed hostel is struggling to survive: please
respect its rules, leave it cleaner than you found it, and treat it with
loving care. Next door is the **pension** (£13 (33 SF) per person,
with room and meals; tel. 55.17.30). (The Gimmelwald grocery
shop is rarely open. Hostelers should bring food with them.)

Up the hill is the treasure of Gimmelwald. Walter Mittler, the
perfect Swiss gentleman, runs a chalet called **Hotel Mittaghorn**.
It's a classic Alpine-style place with a magnificent view of the
Jungfrau Alps. Walter is careful not to let his hotel get too hectic or
too big and enjoys sensitive back-door travellers. He runs his
creaky hotel alone, keeping it simple, but with class. He charges
about £17 (43 SF) for a double with breakfast, single—£10 (26 SF),
dinner—£4.80 (12 SF), and has a loft with cheaper beds. (Address:
3826 Gimmelwald, Bern, Switzerland tel. 036/55.16.58, English
spoken.)

Other good budget beds are at **Masenlager Stocki** (Lauterbrunnen, tel. 55.17.54); dormitory beds at the **Schutzenbach
Campsite**—£4.80 (12 SF) each in four-to-six-bed rooms without
sheets, self-cooking facilities, tel. 036/55.12.68; just past Lauterbrunnen, **Naturfreundehaus Alpenhof** (Stechelberg, 55.12.02);
and the **Chalet Schweizerheim Garni** (£12-£14 (30-35 SF) per
person with breakfast, Wengen, tel. 55.15.81). Younger travellers
love the cheap, American-oriented Balmer's Herberge in Interlaken
(Hauptstr. 23, in Matten, tel. 036/22.19.61). Nearby towns have
plenty of budget accommodation. Let each village's tourist office
help you.

TOUR 18

ALPINE WALKING DAY

If the weather is decent, set today aside for walking. The best walk is from Mannlichen to Kleine Scheidegg to Wengen. Get an early start, when the lifts are cheaper and the weather is usually better. Weather can change rapidly, so always carry a jumper and raingear; wear good walking shoes.

Recommended plan: Leave early. Take the lift to Mürren, take the train to Grutschalp, the funicular down to Lauterbrunnen, then cross the street and catch the train up to Wengen. Do any necessary banking or picnic shopping. Catch the cable car to Mannlichen. Walk to the little peak for a grand view, then around to Kleine Scheidegg for lunch. There's a cafeteria and a restaurant, or you can picnic. To check the weather before investing in a ticket, phone 55.10.22. If you've got an extra £25 (60 SF) and the weather is perfect, take the train through the Eiger to the towering Jungfraujoch and back.

From Kleine Scheidegg, enjoy the ever-changing Alpine panorama of the North Face of the Eiger, Jungfrau and Mönch, probably accompanied by the valley-filling mellow sound of alphorns, as you walk gradually downhill (two hours) to the town of

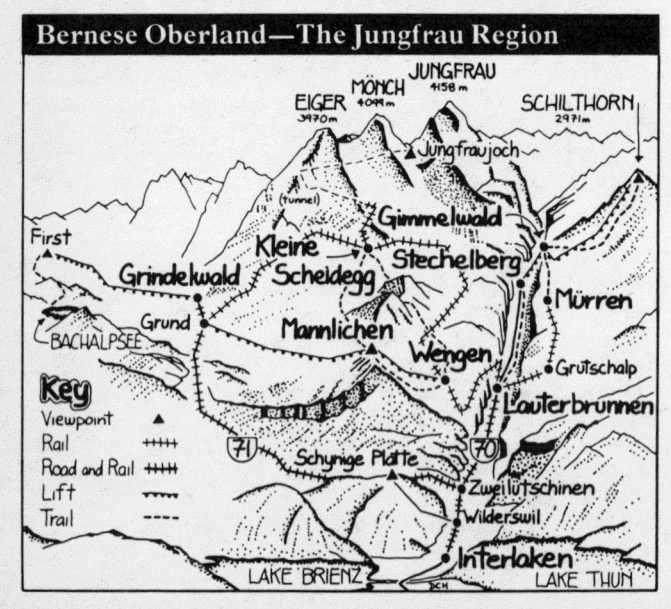

Wengen. If the weather turns bad or you run out of steam, you can catch the train earlier. The trail is very good and the walk is easy for any fit person.

Wengen is a good shopping town. Avoid the steep and boring final descent by catching the train from Wengen to Lauterbrunnen. Travel back up to Grutschalp, take the scenic train or walk to Mürren, and walk back down to Hotel Mittaghorn (45 minutes). Total cost of today's lifts—around £15 (35 SF).

Evening fun in Gimmelwald is found up at Walter's where the local farmers gather to drink, make music and play the spoons. If you're staying at Walter's, don't miss his dinner. Then sit on his porch and watch the sun lick the mountaintops to bed as the moon rises over the Jungfrau.

TOUR 19

FREE TIME IN THE ALPS, EVENING DRIVE INTO FRANCE

If the weather's good, take another walk. The Schilthorn offers the most Alpine excitement around and a memorable breakfast at 10,000 feet. Early in the afternoon it's time to move on, driving out of the Alps, possibly via the Swiss capital Bern, and into France's Alsace region to Colmar—a while new world.

Suggested Schedule

7:30	Catch cable car to Shilthorn.
8:00	The 10,000-foot breakfast.
9:00	Free in Alps to walk or shop in Mürren.
12:00	Picnic in Mürren or back at Walter's.
13:00	Cable car to Stechelberg, drive to Bern.
14:00	Explore Bern.
16:00	Drive into France, stay in Colmar.

Transport

If you're driving, by early afternoon you should be speeding out of the mountains, past the Swiss capital of Bern and on towards Basel, where Switzerland, Germany and France snuggle.

Before Basel you'll go through a tunnel and come to Restatte Pratteln Nord, a strange orange structure that looks like a huge submarine laying eggs on the motorway. Park here for a look around one of Europe's greatest motorway service areas: there's a bakery and grocery shop for picnickers, a restaurant, and a change desk open daily until 21:00 (rates just a little below banks). Spend some time playing around, then carry on (Interlaken to Colmar is a four-hour drive). From Basel follow the signs to France. In France, head north to Colmar, where you can park in the huge square called Place Rapp, and check into the nearby Hôtel Le Rapp. Wander around the old town, then savour an Alsatian meal with the local wine.

Sightseeing Highlights

● ● ●**The 10,000-foot breakfast**—Walter serves a great breakfast, but if the weather's good, skip his and eat on top of the Schilthorn, at 10,000 feet, in a slowly revolving mountain-capping restaurant (of James Bond film fame). The early-bird special

The Gimmelwald Side of Lauterbrunnen Valley

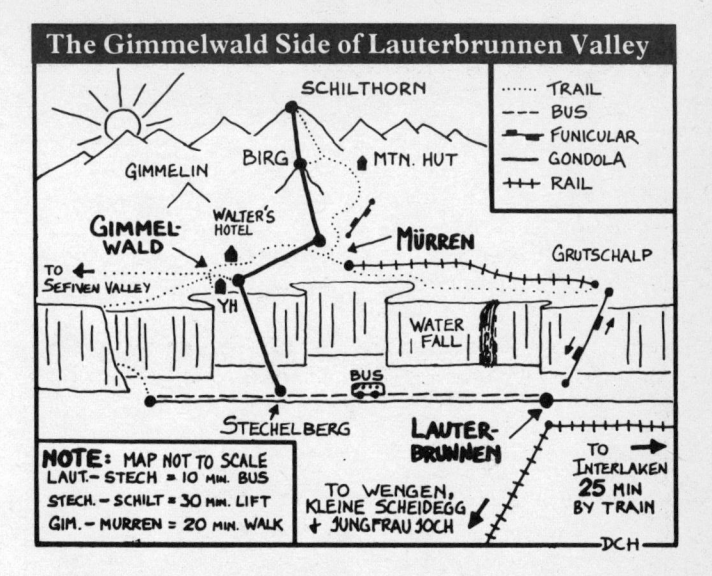

Map legend:
- .... TRAIL
- - - - BUS
- ━╼━ FUNICULAR
- ──── GONDOLA
- +++ RAIL

NOTE: MAP NOT TO SCALE
LAUT. - STECH = 10 MIN. BUS
STECH. - SCHILT = 30 MIN. LIFT
GIM. - MÜRREN = 20 MIN. WALK

cable car tickets (before 9:00) take you from Gimmelwald to the Schilthorn and back with a great continental breakfast on top for about £20 (50 SF). Get tickets at the cable car station or from Walter. Try the Birchermuesli-yogurt treat. Take the lift back down to Mürren, and buy a picnic.

For walkers: The cable car (Gimmelwald-Schilthorn-Gimmelwald) normally costs about £20 (50 SF). The walk (G-S-G) is free, if you don't mind a 5,000-foot altitude gain. Take the cable car up and walk down or, for a less scary walk, go up and halfway down by cable car, then take the steep walk down from the Birg station. Lifts go twice an hour and the journey takes 30 minutes. (The early-bird excursion fare is cheaper than Gimmelwald-Schilthorn-Birg. If you buy the ticket, you can decide at Birg if you want to walk or take the cable car down.) Linger on top. Watch hang gliders get ready, psych themselves up and take off, flying 30 or 40 minutes with the birds to distant Interlaken. Walk along the ridge at the back. You can even convince yourself you climbed to that perch and feel pretty rugged. Think twice before descending from the Schilthorn (weather can change; wear strong shoes). Most people will have more fun walking down from Birg. Just below Birg is a mountain hut. Drop in for soup, cocoa, or a coffee-schnapps. You can spend the night for £2.80 (7 SF) (tel. 036/55.26.40).

The most interesting trail from Mürren to Gimmelwald is the high one via Gimmlin. Consider the walk past Gimmelwald up the

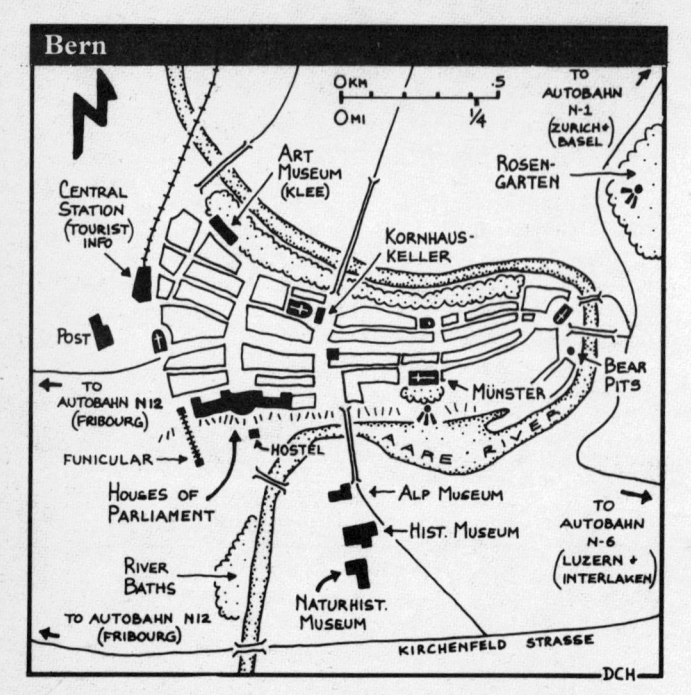

Bern map with labels: To Autobahn N-1 (Zurich, Basel); Art Museum (Klee); Rosengarten; Central Station (Tourist Info); Kornhaus-Keller; Post; To Autobahn N12 (Fribourg); Münster; Bear Pits; Funicular; Hostel; Aare River; Houses of Parliament; Alp Museum; Hist. Museum; To Autobahn N-6 (Luzern & Interlaken); River Baths; Naturhist. Museum; To Autobahn N12 (Fribourg); Kirchenfeld Strasse.

romantic Sefiven Valley. Mürren has plenty of shops, bakeries, tourist information, banks, and a modern sports complex.

● ● **Bern**—The charming Swiss capital fills a peninsula bounded by the Aar River, giving you the most enjoyable look at urban Switzerland. Just an hour from Interlaken, directly on your way to Colmar, it's worth a stop, especially if disappointing weather cuts your mountain time short.

For a short, well-organised visit, park your car at the station, visit the tourist office inside (open 8:00-20:30 daily, till 18:30 in winter, tel. 03/22.76.76), pick up a map and list of city sights, and confirm your plans. Follow the walking tour explained in the handy city map while browsing your way downhill. Finish with a look at the bear pits or *graben* and a city view from the Rose Garden across the river, and catch tram No. 12 back up to the station.

● ● **Highlights of French Switzerland**—The charms of French Switzerland are just a short drive south from Bern. These include Lake Geneve (Lac Leman) with its evocative Chateau Chillon, the resort and jazz city of Montreux, the fascinating Lausanne, the little Geuerien folk museum in Bulle, the fortified village of Gruyeres with its cheese demonstrations, Murten, the best-preserved medieval fortified town in the country, and the mouthwatering Caillers Chocolate factory tours in Broc (9:00 to 10:00 and 13:30 to 15:00 Monday afternoon to Friday morning; tel. 029/61212).

● ●**Ballenberg Swiss Open Air Folk Museum**—If the weather in the Alps is bad, or you happen to hate mountains, try this: The Lauterbrunnen-Interlaken train (£3.20 (8 SF), 30-minutes, goes frequently) will zip you into the big town resort of the region. Interlaken has lots of resort activities and shopping. At the other end of Lake Brienz is Switzerland's best open-air folk museum, Ballenberg (open 9:30-17:30 daily, accessible by train). It's the best possible look at Swiss folklore, with 50 acres of old traditional buildings from all over the country gathered together and displaying the old culture.

Itinerary Options

From Interlaken you can do minor surgery on your itinerary, skip Alsace entirely, and go directly to Paris (excellent overnight train, 22:07-6:18, or all-day drive).

Or, if you're saving France for a later trip, it would be interesting to wander back to Amsterdam via more of Switzerland, the Bodensee, the Black Forest, Trier, Mosel Valley, Luxembourg, Brussels and Bruges. This is mostly small-town and countryside travel so it's best for car travellers.

Or, you may decide to sell your plane ticket and permanently join Heidi and the cows waiting for eternity in Europe's greatest cathedral—the Swiss Alps.

France

■ 210,000 square miles (Western Europe's largest country).
■ 55 million people (248 per square mile, 78 per cent urban).
■ You may have heard that the French are mean and cold. Don't believe it. If anything, they're pouting because they're no longer the world's premier culture. Be sensitive and
understanding. The French are cold only if you choose to perceive them that way. Look for friendliness, give people the benefit of the doubt, respect all that's French and you'll remember France with a smile.
■ At one time the world's most powerful country, France has much to offer in so many ways. Paris will overwhelm you if you don't do a little studying. And Paris is just the beginning of Europe's largest and most diverse country.
■ Learn some French—at least the polite words—and try to sound like Maurice Chevalier. The French don't speak much English—but they speak much more English than we speak French. Unless you speak French, you'll have to be patient about any communications problems.

France

■ The French are experts in the art of fine living. Their cuisine, their customs, even their holiday habits, are highly developed. Since the holiday is such a big part of the French lifestyle (nearly every worker takes either July or August off), you'll find no shortage of tourist information centres, hotels, transport facilities and fun ways to pass free days.

■ The French eat lunch from 12:00 to 14:00, dinner from 19:00 to 22:00—and eat well. A restaurant meal, never rushed, is the day's main event. Each region has its specialities, and even the 'low cuisine' of a picnic can be elegant, with fresh bread and an endless variety of tasty French cheeses, meats, rich pastries and, of course, wine. The best approach to French food is to eat where locals eat and be adventurous. Eat ugly things with relish!

■ France is a reasonably-priced place to travel (plenty of £15 double rooms) and a shopper's delight. Visitors are consistently lured away from important sights by important savings on luxury items, high fashions, perfume, antiques, and tourist trinkets ranging from glow-in-the-dark necklaces to fake gargoyles.

■ French hotels are not as cheap or carefully regulated as in the past. A few tips are helpful. Double beds are cheaper than twins, showers cheaper than baths, breakfast in the dining room, while handy, will cost you about double what the cafe down the street charges (cheaper yet if you stand). Each hotel is rated by stars on a plaque near its door. The star system indicates general standards and price; in Paris * = £10-£15 (100-150F) per double, ** = £15-£30 (150-300F) per double, *** = £30-£40 (300-400F) per double. Countryside prices are substantially less. If you're on a budget, ask for cheaper rooms.

■ French Money: The French franc (FF or F) is divided into 100 centimes (c). A franc is worth about 10p. There are 10 francs in a pound. So, divide prices by 10 to get pounds (eg. 65F = £6.50).

■ Public telephones. France's nearly extinct coin-operated public telephones are being replaced by super efficient, vandal-resistant, card-operated models. Upon entry into France, buy a phone card from a post office or *tabac* shop and take advantage of the phone. Smallest card is £4 (40F). To use the phone booths (which you should for hotels and restaurant reservation and confirmation, tourist and train information, museum hours, phoning home, etc.), the little screen will instruct you to: 1) Pick up receiver, 2) 'Introduce' card, 3) 'Closez le lid' over your card, 4) Have 'patientez', 5) The amount of money you have will show on the little screen (e.g. credit: 4.80F), 6) Dial your 'numéro'. After you hang up 'retirez' your card. You've got coin-free use of the French telephone system until your card expires.

Eating and Sleeping

In general, France is wonderful for the budget traveller. Any one-star or two-star hotel (indicated by a blue-and-white plaque near the door) will offer bed and breakfast for £6-£10 (60-100F) per person. Popular Colmar and Alsace can be difficult in peak season so, as usual, it's wise to arrive early or phone ahead.

Hôtel Le Rapp in Colmar is ideal (Rue Berthe-Molly, tel. 3389/41-62-10 from another country or 89/41-62-10 from France). Friendly, intimate, with a great local restaurant, £16 (160F) doubles, English spoken. It's run by Bernard, who mixes class with warmth like no man I've met. If he's full, ask him for a recommendation. **Hôtel Turenne** (10 Rt. de Bâle, tel. 89/41-12-26) and **La Chaumière** (74 Av. de la République, tel. 41-08-99) are also good. The tourist information office, too, can find you a room. Nearby towns and villages aren't so crowded and can offer an even more Alsatian hotel experience. But Colmar is your best headquarters town.

The best budget beds in Colmar are at the **Maison des Jeunes** (Camille-Schlumberger 17, near the station in a comfortable and fairly central location, tel. 89/41-26-87). The desk is open from

14:00-23:00. A bed in a large room costs about £3 (30F). The **youth hostel** (Rue St. Niklaus 6, a brisk 15-minute walk down Av. de la Liberté from the station, tel. 89/41-33-08) offers £3.40 (34F) beds from March to October.

Alsatian cuisine is great. Many visitors come here only to eat. Bernard's restaurant in **Hôtel Le Rapp** is my dress-up, haute-cuisine meal of the tour: several great fixed menus from 4.40 (44F) to £11.70 (117F). Comb your hair, change your socks and savour a slow, elegant meal served with grace and fine wine. Don't miss the Salade Rapp. For crêpes with atmosphere—**Crêperie Tom Pouce**, 10 Rue des Tanneurs, tel. 23-27-00. For cheap, low-risk, low-stress meals, eat at the **Flunch** self-service in Place Rapp or in the fine cafeteria at **Monoprix** near the Unterlinden Museum. The **Rutabaga** vegetarian restaurant just around the corner from Hotel Le Rapp and **A la Fleur** (at Rue du Consul Souvernin 3, closed Tues. and Wed.) are two more good value eating places.

TOUR 20

COLMAR, ALSATIAN VILLAGES, WINE TASTING

After Bernard's breakfast, a morning free to explore Colmar, and a cafeteria lunch at Flunch (a great French self-service cafeteria chain), wander the Route du Vin (France's wine road) and visit the villages of Eguisheim and Kaysersberg. Call in at a winery in either town for a tour and tasting before returning to Hôtel le Rapp for a memorable evening dose of Alsatian cuisine.

Suggested Schedule

8:00	Breakfast
8:30	Orientation walk through old Colmar, ending at tourist office.
9:00	Unterlinden Museum (don't miss the Issenheim altarpiece).
10:30	Free time in Colmar to shop, sightsee, wash or write letters.
13:00	Lunch at Flunch or picnic in a village.
14:00	Exploration of France's wine road and villages, with a winery tour and tasting.
19:30	Find your way back to Colmar for a tasty Alsatian dinner at Hotel Le Rapp.

Sightseeing Highlights

●●●**Unterlinden Museum**—Colmar's touristic claim to fame, this is one of my favourite museums in Europe. Its extensive yet manageable collection ranges from Roman Colmar to medieval wine-making exhibits to traditional wedding dresses to babies' cribs to Picasso. Even if you're feeling 'museumed-out' at this point in your trip, don't miss Grünewald's gripping Issenheim Altarpiece. Pick up the English guidebook at the desk, study the polyptych model of the multi-panelled painting on the wall near the original, and get acquainted with this greatest of late-medieval German masterpieces. Open 9:00-18:00 daily, £1.70 (17F).

●●**Dominican Church**—Here another medieval mind-blower awaits your attention. In Colmar's Dominican church you'll find Martin Schongauer's angelically beautiful Virgin of the Roses, looking as though it was painted yesterday, holding court on centre stage (open 10:00-18:00 daily, 5F). On many evenings you can enjoy its 13th-century stained glass lit from inside.

Colmar

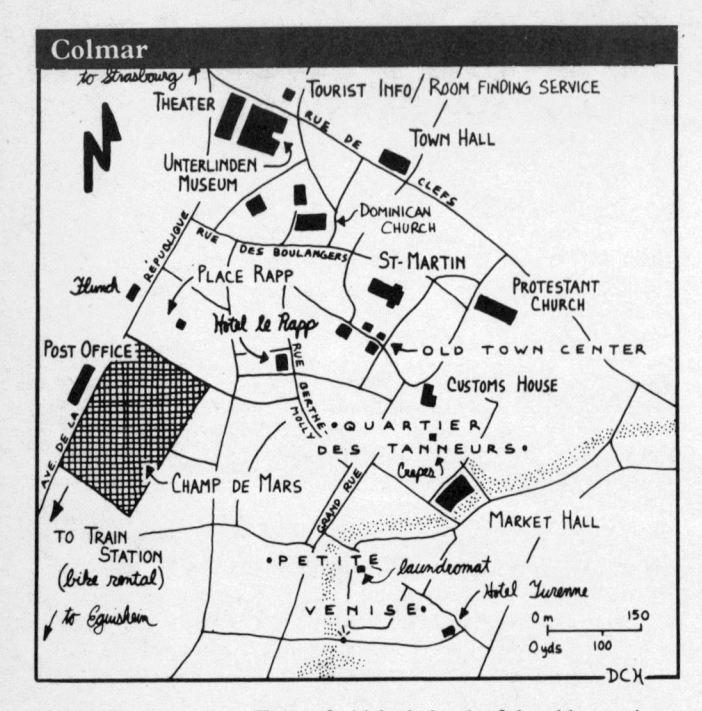

[Map of Colmar showing: to Strasbourg, Theater, Tourist Info/Room Finding Service, Town Hall, Rue de Clefs, Unterlinden Museum, Rue République, Rue des Boulangers, Dominican Church, St-Martin, Place Rapp, Protestant Church, Flunch, Hotel le Rapp, Rue Bertha, Old Town Center, Post Office, Rue Nelly, Customs House, Quartier des Tanneurs, Ave de la, Champ de Mars, Grand Rue, Crêperie, Market Hall, to Train Station (bike rental), to Eguisheim, Petite Venise, laundromat, Hotel Turenne. Scale: 0m-150, 0yds-100. — DCH]

Tanners' Quarters—This refurbished chunk of the old town is a delight, day or night. A good crêperie is at 10 Rue des Tanneurs.
Bartholdi Museum—An interesting little museum about the life and work of the local boy who gained fame by sculpting the Statue of Liberty. You'll notice several of his statues, usually with one arm raised high, gracing Colmar's squares.
●●**Route du Vin Side Trip**—Alsace has so much to offer. If you have only one afternoon, limit yourself to these two towns:
Eguisheim—Just a few miles from Colmar, this scenic little town is best explored by walking around its circular road, then cutting through the middle. Visit the Eguisheim Wine Cooperative.
Kaysersberg—Albert Schweitzer's home town is larger but just as quaint as Eguisheim. Climb the castle, browse through the art galleries, enjoy the colourful bundle of 15th-century houses near the fortified town bridge, visit Dr. Schweitzer's house, see the church with its impressive 400-year-old altar-piece, taste some wine and wander along nearby vineyards. (Tourist office tel. 89/78-22-78.)
***Dégustation* along France's Wine Road**—Throughout Alsace you'll see '*Dégustation*' signs. *Dégustation* means 'come on in and taste', and *gratuit* means 'free' (otherwise there's a very small

Alsace & Black Forest

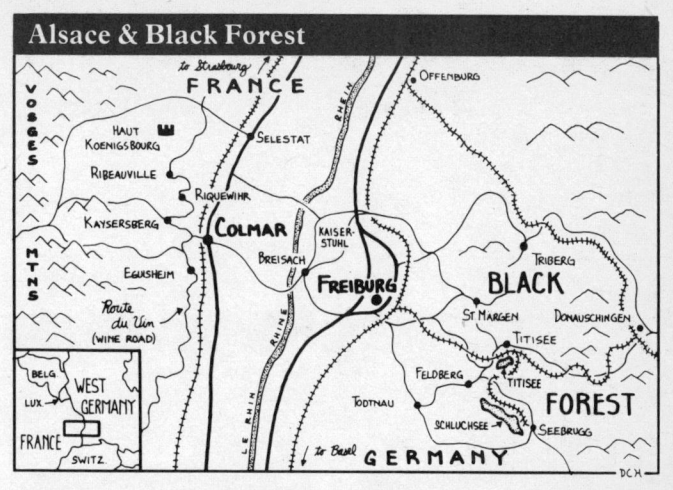

charge). Most towns have wineries that give tours. The Eguisheim Wine Cooperative is good; the town of Bennwihr has a modern cooperative created after the destruction of World War II, which gives a fascinating look at a more modern and efficient method of production. Your hotel receptionist or the people at the tourist office can give you advice or even telephone a winery for you to confirm tour times. You may have to wait for a group and tag along for a tour and free tasting. Be sure to try *Crémant*, the Alsatian 'champagne'. It's very good—and much cheaper. Ask about wine festivals or local out-door wine tastings in Colmar. September is a particularly festive harvest season. (The French words for headache, if you really get 'Alsaced', are *mal à la tête*.)

Many enjoy hiring a bike at the Colmar station for their wine road excursion (go easy on the tasting).

Helpful Hints

Old Colmar is easily covered on foot. Worthwhile guidebooks are in most gift shops, and the tourist office (tel. 89/41-02-29) can provide maps, hours, tours of the Route du Vin, a private guide (£18 (180F), summers only), and general information and ideas for your trip into the wine road region.

Colmar is a good place for posting things if your parcel is under about 10 pounds. (Posting in Paris can be a headache.) The post office near Place Rapp sells boxes, is open 8:00-19:00, has postal clerks as cheery and speedy as yours at home, and is a good place to lighten your load. Colmar is also a good place to do laundry (self-service launderette at 8 Rue des Tanneurs, daily 8:00-21:00) and to shop (shops close Monday mornings).

TOUR 21

THE LONG DRIVE TO PARIS, STOPPING AT REIMS

This journey will take you halfway across France to Paris, with a stop for lunch, a champagne tour, and a visit to a great Gothic cathedral in Reims. You can be in Paris in time for dinner, a metro lesson and a city orientation tour.

Suggested Schedule

7:00	Leave Colmar. Breakfast at service area.
12:00	Reims—picnic, tour cathedral and champagne cave.
14:00	Drive to Paris.
17:00	Arrive in Paris.

Transport

Drivers: leave Colmar by 7:00, head north past Strasbourg and take the *autoroute* straight to Reims (five hours). You'll pass Verdun (an interesting stop for history and World War I buffs) and lots of strange, modern Franco-motorway art.

Take the Reims exit marked 'Cathedral' and you'll see your destination. Park near the church. Picnic in the park near its front (public toilet, dangerous grass, glorious setting). Back on the *autoroute*, it's a straight drive (except for toll-booths) into Paris. By this schedule, you should arrive just about rush hour (no tour is perfect).

If you're hiring a car it would be better to return it at Charles de Gaulle airport and get into town by catching the airport bus to the nearest metro station. Or phone your hotel from Reims and ask if you can arrive late. Or just damn the torpedoes, think of it as London: fasten your seatbelt, check your insurance, and drive. If you're in danger of going 'in-Seine', hire a taxi and follow him to your hotel. If you think you're good behind the wheel, drive this introductory tour as the sun sets: go over the Austerlitz Bridge, to the Luxembourg Gardens, down Boulevard St. Michel, past Notre-Dame on the island, up the Champs-Elysées, around the Arc de Triomphe (six or eight giggly times) and to your hotel. Confirm your hotel reservation upon arrival or earlier in the day by telephone.

By train you can connect from Colmar to Reims to Paris easily, but I'd probably skip Reims, save a day, and take the train

Reims Cathedral

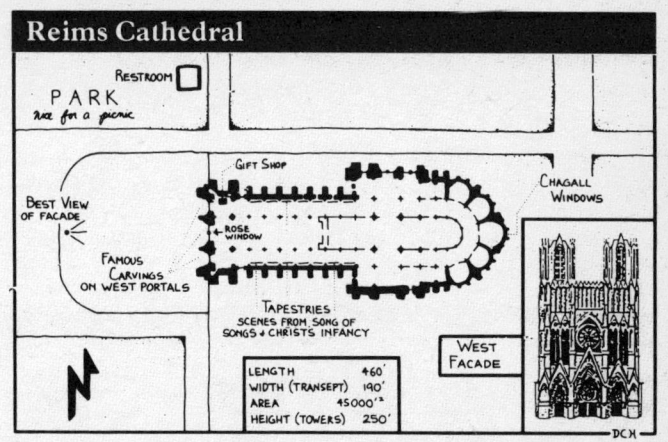

[Map of Reims Cathedral showing: Park (nice for a picnic), Restroom, Gift Shop, Chagall Windows, Best View of Facade, Rose Window, Famous Carvings on West Portals, Tapestries (Scenes from Song of Songs & Christs Infancy), West Facade. Dimensions: Length 460', Width (transept) 190', Area 45000'², Height (towers) 250'.]

overnight from nearby Basel to Paris (00:10-6:48) or the direct five-hour journey during the day. Chartres Cathedral, an hour from Paris, is as good as Reims.

Reims

The cathedral of Reims is one of the best examples of Gothic architecture you'll see. For 800 years it was the coronation place of French kings and queens. It houses many old treasures, not to mention a lovely modern set of Marc Chagall stained glass windows. (Open 8:00-21:00 daily.)

Reims is the capital of the Champagne region and, while the bubbly stuff's birthplace was Epernay, it's best to save nearly two hours of road time by touring a champagne cave right in Reims. Walk ten minutes up Rue de Barbatre from the Cathedral to 9 Place St. Nicaise (tel. 26/85-45-35), where the Taittinger Company will do a great job trying to convince you they're the best. After seeing their film (the comfy theatre seats alone make this a worthwhile visit), follow your guide down into some of the three miles of chilly chalk caves, many dug by ancient Romans. Popping corks signal when the tour's done and the tasting's begun.

One block beyond Taittinger, in Place des Droits de l'Homme, you'll find several other champagne firms. Most give free tours Monday to Saturday from 9:00-11:00 and 14:00-17:00. I'd recommend Piper Heidsieck, with its tacky train tour (51 Bd. Henry-Vasnier, call first at tel. 26/85-01-94), and Veuve Clicquot-Pousardin (1 Place des Droits de l'Homme, tel. 26/85-24-08). If you want to drive to Epernay (nice town, plenty of cheap hotels) the best champagne firm with the best tours (free, 45 minutes, in English, samples) is right in town: Moët et Chandon. (20 Av. de Champagne, tel. 26/54-71-11, open daily with a break for lunch.)

TOUR 22

PARIS

Paris provides a grand finale for this trip: There's no city in Europe so magnificent. Paris is sweeping boulevards, sleepy parks, staggering art galleries, friendly crêpe stands, Napoleon's body and sleek shopping malls, the Eiffel Tower and people-watching from an outdoor cafe. Many people fall in love with Paris. Many see the Mona Lisa and flee disappointed. With the proper approach and a good orientation, you'll be one of the lucky ones who fall in love with Europe's capital city.

Suggested Schedule

8:00	Breakfast.
8:30	Metro to St. Michel in Latin Quarter.
9:00	Walk through Latin Quarter to Notre-Dame.
9:30	Tour Notre-Dame.
10:00	Deportation Memorial.
10:30	Tour Sainte Chapelle.
11:30	Lunch at 5th floor Samaritaine department store cafeteria.
13:00	Tour the Louvre, hopefully with a guide.
16:00	Stroll through the Tuileries and up the Champs-Elysées to the Arc de Triomphe.
19:30	Dinner in Latin Quarter along Rue Mouffetard.
Additionally (or Alternatively)	
9:00	Shopping at les Halles.
10:30	Tour the Orsay Museum.
14:00	Cruise the Seine.
16:00	Up the Eiffel Tower.
19:00	Evening in Montmartre.

Orientation

Paris stretches forever, but our Paris is the old core, clustered around the island in the Seine River where the city was born 300 years before Christ. The Seine River divides the city into the Right bank (North, Louvre, Opéra, Arc de Triomphe, Sacré-Coeur) and the Left bank (South, Latin Quarter, Eiffel Tower).

Paris is divided into 20 *arrondissements* (or districts) which spiral clockwise out from the island. Addresses include the district. The 18th arrondissement would be '*18ème*' or the last two numbers of the postal code (e.g. 75018). Directions also include the nearest metro stop. ('Mo: Opéra' means it's near the Opéra stop.)

Your key to enjoying Paris is mastering its excellent metro system. The Paris Metro is Europe's best. One ticket takes you anywhere, much faster than a car or taxi, for only 30p (3F); buy tickets in books of ten (*carnet*) for big savings. There are also special two-, four- and seven-day passes which you can purchase locally. The Paris metro is easy if you have a city map (available free at any hotel or metro station) and knows that *sortie* means exit and *correspondance* means 'go this way to make a connection'. Directions are indicated by the last stop on that line.

If possible, use the RER train system. It's much, much faster, and metro tickets are accepted. It's ideal for connecting Paris's mainline stations and getting out to Versailles. Parisian buses are slow but great fun. Buses 21, 69, 95, and 96 are each very scenic (metro tickets work on buses).

Take a day to cover the core sights of Paris and get comfortable with the city in general.

Start by taking the metro to the St. Michel stop where you'll emerge in the heart of the Latin Quarter. This is a lively place at night; it uses mornings to recover. Walk down Rue de la Huchette (past the popular jazz cellar at 5—check the schedule) and over the bridge to Notre-Dame cathedral. It took 200 years to build this church: tour it accordingly. Walk around to the impressive back of the church (pleasant park, impressive buttresses). Then pass through the tour coach park to the tip of the island to visit the moving memorial to the 200,000 French people deported by Hitler in World War II. Walking through the centre of the island, Ile de la Cité, you'll come to the Sainte-Chapelle church, newly restored, a Gothic gem. Walk to the northeast tip of the island (lovely park) and cross (to the right) the oldest bridge in town, the Pont-Neuf to the Samaritaine department store. Have lunch on its fifth floor (cafeteria open 11:30-15:00, 15:30-18:30).

Then your time has come to tackle the Louvre. Europe's one-time grandest palace and biggest building houses its greatest—and most overwhelming—museum. The new Louvre entrance is a grand modern glass pyramid in the central courtyard.

For the rest of the afternoon, take a leisurely, people-watching walk through the Tuileries Gardens up the Champs-Elysées to the Arc de Triomphe (small museum on top with a great city view).

Paris's main (and very crowded) tourist office is at No. 127 in the Champs-Elysées, open daily from 9:00 to 20:00, tel. 47/23-61-72. There are also tourist offices at each station.

The Heart of Paris

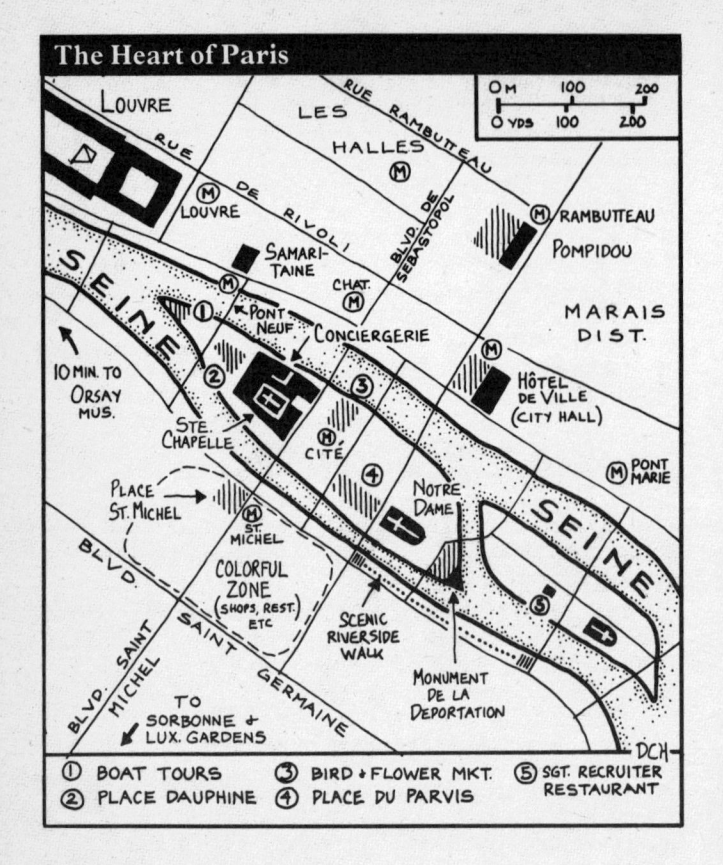

[Map showing central Paris with landmarks including the Louvre, Les Halles, Rambuteau/Pompidou, Marais District, Hôtel de Ville (City Hall), Pont Marie, Samaritaine, Pont Neuf, Conciergerie, Ste. Chapelle, Cité, Notre Dame, Place St. Michel, Colorful Zone (shops, rest., etc), Scenic Riverside Walk, Monument de la Deportation, Blvd. Saint Michel, Saint Germaine, to Sorbonne & Lux. Gardens, and the Seine. Numbered points: ① Boat Tours, ② Place Dauphine, ③ Bird & Flower Mkt., ④ Place du Parvis, ⑤ Sgt. Recruiter Restaurant. 10 min. to Orsay Mus.]

Sightseeing Highlights

●●**Latin Quarter**—This area lies between the Luxembourg Gardens and the island centring around the Sorbonne university and Boulevards St. Germain and St. Michel. This is the core of the Left Bank—the arty, liberal, hippie, Bohemian, poet and philosopher district. It's full of international eateries, way-out bookshops, street singers and jazz clubs. For colourful wandering and cafe-sitting, afternoons and evenings are best.

●●**Notre-Dame Cathedral**—700 years old, packed with history and tourists. Climb to the top (entrance on outside left, open 10:00-17:30) for a great gargoyle's eye view of the city. Study its sculpture (Notre-Dame's forte) and stained-glass windows, take in a musical service (or the free Sunday 17:45 recital on the 6,000-pipe organ, France's largest), eavesdrop on guides, walk all around the outside. Open 8:00-19:00. Ask about the free English tours (normally August only). Treasury open 10:00-18:00.

● ●**Deportation Memorial**—Don't miss the powerful memorial to the French victims of the Holocaust. The design and architecture— water, sky, bars, and concrete eternal flame—the names of many concentration camps, and a crystal for each of the 200,000 lost ones, is very effective. (On the tip of the island near Ile St. Louis, behind Notre-Dame, opens at 10:00, free.)

● ● ●**Sainte-Chapelle**—The triumph of Gothic church architecture, a cathedral of glass like none other, it was built in just 33 months to house the Crown of Thorns—which cost the king more than the church. Newly restored. Good little book with colour photos available in English (£2.20 (22F)). Open 10:00-18:00. Concerts almost every evening (£9 (90F)). Even a beginners' violin class would sound lovely in that atmospheric room. Tel. 43/54-30-09.

● ● ●**The Louvre**—Europe's oldest, biggest, greatest—and maybe most crowded—museum. Take a tour or buy the square little guidebook. Don't try to cover it thoroughly. Open 9:45-18:30 (some sections close 11:30-14:00). Closed Tuesday. Free (and more crowded) on Sunday. Tel. info 42/86-99-00. English tours normally leave at 10:15, 11:30 and 15:30. Buy a combination guided tour-admission ticket; a tour is the best way to enjoy this huge museum. (*Mona Winks* includes self-guided tours of the Louvre, the Orsay, the Pompidou, and Versailles.)

If you're unable to get a guide, a good do-it-yourself tour of the museum's highlights would include (in this order): ancient Greek, Parthenon frieze, Venus de Milo, Nike of Samothrace, Apollo Gallery (jewels), French paintings found between the Nike of Samothrace and the Grande Galerie, the Grande Galerie (a quarter of a mile long and worth the walk), the Mona Lisa and her room-mates, the nearby Neo-classical collection (Coronation of Napoleon, by David) and the Romantic collection (Delacroix and Gericault).

● ● ●**Orsay Museum**—This is Paris's long-awaited '19th-century' art museum (actually art from 1848-1914) including Europe's greatest collection of Impressionism. This style is often hard to appreciate without a tour. On the ground floor: Conservative-establishment 'pretty' art on right; cross the tracks into the brutally truthful and, at the time, very shocking art of the rebels and Manet. Then go up the escalator at the far end to the series of Impressionist rooms and Van Gogh. Don't miss the Art Nouveau on the mezzanine level. The museum is housed in a former railway station across the river and ten minutes downstream from the Louvre. Tel. 45/49-48-14, Open 10:30-18:00, Thurs. until 21:45, closed Mon. £2.50 (25F).

Paris

1 HOTELS AROUND RUE CLER	2 COLORFUL BUDGET HOTEL AREA: RUE MOUFFETARD	3 SAMARITAINE DEPT STORE - SELF SERVE REST. 4 JAZZ CLUB - CAVEAU DE LA HUCHETTE
5 MEMORIAL DE LA DEPORTATION	6 GARE INVALIDES - DIRECT RER TRAIN TO VERSAILLES	

● **Napoleon's Tomb** and the **Army Museum**—The Emperor lies majestically dead under a grand dome, a goose-bumping pilgrimage for historians, surrounded by the tombs of other French war heroes and Europe's greatest military museum (in the Hôtel des Invalides). Open daily 10:00-18:00, Sun 9:00-18:00.

● **Rodin Museum**—Work of the greatest sculptor since Michelangelo. This museum is filled with surprisingly entertaining sculpture: The Kiss, The Thinker, and many more. Just across the street from Napoleon's Tomb. (Open 10:00-17:45, closed Tues.)

● **Pompidou Centre**—This controversial, colourfully exoskeletal building houses Europe's greatest collection of modern art, the Musée National d'Art Moderne. You'll find fun art, such as a piano smashed to bits and glued to the wall. It's a social centre with lots of people. There's activity inside and out, swamped by a perpetual street fair. (Open noon-22:00, Sat. and Sun. 10:00-22:00, closed Tues., free on Sun. tel. 42/77-12-33)

● ● **Eiffel Tower**—Crowded and expensive, Europe's most famous tower is worth the trouble. Open daily 10:00-23:00. £1.10 (11F) first level, £2.80 (28F) second, £4.40 (44F) to go all the way for the 1,000-foot view. I think the view from the 400-foot-high second level is plenty. Pilier Nord (the north pillar) has the biggest lift, so its queue moves fastest. The Restaurant Belle-France (first level) serves decent £6 (60F) meals. Don't miss the entertaining and free history-of-the-tower film on the first level.

● ●**Montparnasse Tower**—This 59-floor superscraper is cheaper and easier to get to the top of than the Eiffel Tower. Buy the photo-guide to the city, go to the rooftop for possibly Paris's best view, and orientate yourself. This is the best way to understand the lay of this magnificent land. It's a good place to be as the sun goes down on your first day in Paris. Find your hotel, retrace your day's steps, locate the famous buildings. Open summer 9:30-23:00, off-season 10:00-21:45.

●**Samaritaine Department Store Viewpoint**—Go to the rooftop (free, take the lift from near the Pont-Neuf entrance). Quiz yourself. Turn counter-clockwise, identifying the Eiffel Tower, Invalides/Napoleon's Tomb, Montparnasse Tower, Henry IV statue on the island, Sorbonne University, the dome of the Pantheon, Sainte Chapelle, Hôtel de Ville (city hall), the wild and colourful Pompidou Centre, the Byzantine-looking Sacfe Coeur, Opéra and Louvre. Light meals on the breezy terrace and a good self-service restaurant on fourth floor.

● ●**Sacré-Coeur and Montmartre**—This Byzantine-looking church is only 100 years old but it's very impressive. It was built as a praise-the-Lord-anyway gesture after the French were humiliated by the Germans in a brief war in 1871. Nearby is the Place du Tertre, the haunt of Toulouse-Lautrec and the original 'Bohemians'. Today it's mobbed by tourists, but still fun. Watch the artists, tip the street singers, have a dessert crêpe. Church is open daily and evenings. 'Plaster of Paris' comes from the Gypsum found on this 'mont'. (Place Blanche is the white place nearby where they used to load it...sloppily.)

Pigalle—Paris's red-light district. Oo la la! More shocking than dangerous. Stick to the bigger streets, hang on to your wallet and exercise good judgment.

Seine River Tour—A relaxing, if uninspiring, float up and down past a parade of famous buildings, a *bateau-mouche* trip costs £3.50 (35F) and leaves from the Pont-Neuf or near the Eiffel Tower.

Best Shopping—Forum Halles is a grand new subterranean shopping mall, a sight in itself. Fun, mod, colourful, very Parisian (Metro: Halles). The Galeries Lafayette behind the Opera House is your best elegant, old-world one-stop Parisian department-store shopping centre. Also, visit one of several Printemps stores, and the historic Samaritaine department store near Pont-Neuf.

Good Browsing Areas—Rue Rambuteau from the Halles to the Pompidou Centre, the Marais/Jewish Quarter/Place des Vosges area, the Champs-Elysées, and the Latin Quarter.

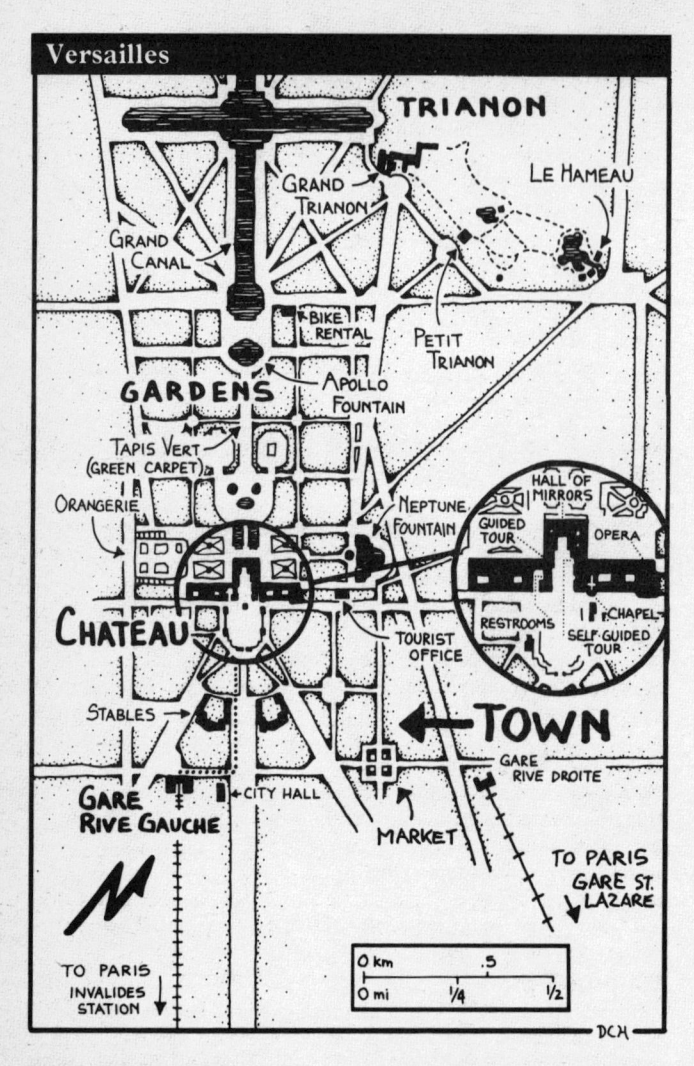

Side Trips

● ● ● **Versailles**—Europe's palace of palaces, Versailles is 12 miles from the centre of Paris. To get there take the metro to Invalides or St. Michel and follow signs to 'Versailles R.G.'. Take that RER train (£1 (10F), free with Eurail, 45 minutes; runs every ten minutes) to the end of the line (Versailles R.G.) and walk ten minutes to the palace. Arrive early or late to avoid the mob

scene. Tour groups seem to arrive in waves, around 11:00 and
around 14:00. Tuesdays are the most crowded. Take the private
'king's apartments' tour immediately to avoid more crowds (use
Guided Tour entrance—see map). Buy the middle-priced guidebook
for a room-by-room rundown. Walk 45 minutes (or hire a bike) to
the Little Hamlet (a great picnic spot). Open Tues.-Sun. 9:45-5:30,
closed Monday. The town of Versailles is quiet and pleasant.
The central market is great for picnic supplies and the cosy crêperie
in Rue des Deux Portes has a crêpe selection that would impress
Louis himself!

● **Chartres**—One of Europe's most important Gothic cathedrals,
one hour by train from Paris. Open 7:00-19:00. Malcolm
Miller gives great 'Appreciation-of-Gothic' tours every day (except
Sunday) at about noon and 14:45; each tour is different. Just
show up at the cathedral. This church is great, but for most people
Notre-Dame in Paris is easier and good enough. Chartres' youth
hostel features a fabulous cathedral view.

● ● ●**The Château of Chantilly** (pron: shan-tee-yee)—France's
best *château* (castle), Chantilly is just 30 minutes (2.90 (29F))
by train from the Paris North Station. You'll find everything
you hoped a château would have—a moat, drawbridge, sculpted
gardens, little hamlet (the prototype for the more famous *hameau* at
Versailles), lavish interior (rivals Versailles) with included English
tour, world-class art collection (including two Raphaels)...and
no crowds. Open daily except Tuesday, 10:00-18:00. £3.50 (35F)
admission includes tour. Horse lovers will enjoy the nearby stables,
literally built for a prince—who believed he'd be reincarnated as
a horse. (On my last visit, I think I worked out which horse is the
prince.) The quaint and impressively preserved medieval town of
Senlis is a 30-minute bus journey from Chantilly station.

Giverny—Monet's garden is very popular with his fans. Open
10:00-12:00, 14:00-18:00, April 1-Oct. 31, closed Monday. Take
Rouen train from St. Lazare Station to Vernon, then walk, hitch or
taxi to Giverny (4 km).

Helpful Hints

Remember, nearly all Paris museums are closed on Tuesdays
(except the Orsay and Versailles which are closed Mondays—and
especially crowded on Tuesdays). Pick up a copy of the weekly
entertainment guide, *Pariscope*, to check the local museum hours
and know what's going on at night. There's a great (but a bit
touristy) jazz club and dancing at the Caveau de la Huchette (5 Rue
de la Huchette, £5.50 (55F) cover, music nightly from 21:30) in
the Latin Quarter. Note that Paris expanded its overworked phone
system, adding a 4 to the beginning of all old numbers.

Eating and Sleeping

Finding rooms in Paris is most difficult in September, October, May and June (conference months). July and August are fairly easy—just don't look for hotels in the shadows of famous buildings. Arrive early or use one of the tourist office room-finding services (tel. 43/59-12-12).

A handy, quiet, central and safe area with a cluster of fine budget hotels is at the metro stop Montmartre (in the ninth district, halfway between the Opera and the Pompidou Centre). Find the quiet alley running between Rue Bergère and Boulevard Poissonnière (30 yards in front of the Flunch and through a corridor on the left.)

My Montmartre recommendations: **Hôtel des Arts** (7 Cité Bergère, 75009 Paris, tel. 42/46-73-30. £26-£28 (260-285F) doubles with showers, high class, some English spoken, friendly). **Hôtel Cité Rougemont** (4 Cité Rougemont, 75009 Paris, tel. 47/70-25-95; three doubles for £15 (150F), doubles with shower or bath £25-£28.50 (250-285F), breakfast— £1.80 (18F), telephone reservations okay, some English, friendly fun). **Hotel d'Espagne** (9 Cité Bergère, tel. 47/70-13-94, doubles for £27-£34 (270-340F).

Another even more comfortable Parisian area to call home is Rue Cler. This village-like pedestrian street is safe, tidy, and makes you feel great to be in Paris. (How such cosiness lodged itself between the stately government-business, high-powered, and expensive Eiffel Tower and Invalides areas, I'll never know.) You can stay in one of the hotels listed below and eat and browse your way through the street full of bright shops, colourful outdoor fruit and vegetable stalls and fish vendors. The metro is a few blocks away (Metro: Ecole Militaire or La-Tour-Maubourg) but buses 28, 42, 49, 63, 69, 80 and 92 stop on the corner. There's a handy post office and a self-service launderette (just off Cler in Rue de Grenelle). **Grand Hôtel Lévêque**, 29 Rue Cler, 75007 Paris, tel. 47/05-49-15, 50 rooms, offers doubles for £16-£26 (160-260F) with breakfast, basic, clean, quiet, some English spoken; will hold a room if you telephone—if they can understand you. **Hôtel du Centre**, 24 Rue Cler, 75007 Paris, tel. 47/05-52-33, 30 rooms, has five cheap doubles at £14 (140F); doubles with showers or bath range from £18-£23 (180-230F), triples with enough plumbing to sink a ship £29.50 (295F). Breakfast £2.30 (23F). No reservations without a deposit. Run by nice people, more fun than the Hôtel Lévêque across the street. **Hôtel La Motte-Picquet**, 30 Av. de la Motte Picquet, tel. 47/05-09-57, on corner of Rue Cler, is more mod, with less character but a TV and mini-bar in each room. 18 doubles all with showers, £22.50-£29.50 (225-295F), breakfast extra. **Hôtel du Champ-de-Mars**, 7 Rue du Champ-de-Mars, tel.

45/51-52-30, has doubles from £26 to £29 (260 to 290F), breakfast extra. **Hotel Rustic**, 2 Rue Duvivier, tel. 47/05-89-27, doubles £18-£20 (180-200F), is a dark, tangled, intriguing place. There's an 'American Bar' in cellar. **Hôtel Amelie**, 5 Rue Amelie, tel. 45/51-74-75,£35 (350F) doubles, is unexceptional, expensive, decent in this good neighbourhood.

Those interested in a more Soho/Greenwich Village gentrified urban-jungle atmosphere would enjoy making the Marais-Jewish Quarter-St. Paul-Vosges area their home in Paris: this is an alive area where you can take the pulse of Paris. The metro stop St. Paul puts you right in the heart of the Marais. Unfortunately, the hotel situation is pretty lean. **Hôtel de la Place des Vosges** is a two-star hotel at 12 Rue de Birague, tel. 42/72-60-46, doubles £25-£33 (250-330F), English spoken, often full so phone ahead, just off the elegant Place des Vosges. **Hôtel Stella**, 14 Rue Neuve Saint-Pierre, tel. 42/72-23-66, is plain and bleak, on a quiet street with decent management. Eight cheap doubles for £12 (120F) each, good value. Rue St. Paul has only one hotel, **Hôtel de l'Art**, with no character and £20-£28 (200-280F) doubles.

Hotels in other areas: **Hôtel International** (6 Rue Auguste-Barbier, metro: Goncourt, 75011 Paris, tel. 43/57-38-07) is very good value, £27 (270F) doubles, in an out-of-the-way but pleasant area. In the Latin Quarter look for cheap decent rooms along Rue des Ecoles. Student travellers should take advantage of the room-finding service at 119 Rue St. Martin near the Pompidou Centre, tel. 42/77-87-80, at the Gare du Nord, at 16 Rue du Pont Louis-Philippe near the Hôtel de Ville, or at 139 Bd. St. Michel in the Latin Quarter.

Eating in Paris

You could eat yourself silly in Paris. The city could hold a gourmets' Olympics—and import nothing. Picnic or go to snack bars for quick lunches, and linger longer over delicious dinners. You can eat very well, restaurant-style, for under £10. Ask your hotel to recommend a small, French restaurant nearby in the 50-to-80F range. Famous places are overpriced, overcrowded, and usually overrated. Find a quiet area and wander or follow a local recommendation: you'll dine well.

Rock-bottom budget choices—self-services and cafeterias: many Parisian department stores have top floor cafeterias. Try **La Samaritaine** at Pont-Neuf near the Louvre, 4th floor. There are several **Flunch** cafeterias around town (just off the Champs-Elysées, near metro shops Montmartre and Clichy). The **Melodine** self-service (metro: Rambuteau, next to Pompidou Centre) is great, open daily 11:00-22:00. **Le Chartier** (7 Rue du Faubourge Montmartre, metro: Montmartre), **Commerce** (51 Rue du

Commerce, metro: Commerce) and **Drouot** (103 Rue de Richelieu, metro: Richelieu-Drouot) all serve very cheap and basic food.

For picnics, you'll find handy little groceries all over town (but rarely near famous sights). The ultimate high-class picnic shopping place is **Fauchon**, the famous 'best gourmet grocery in France'; delicious window displays, top quality, fast, expensive but cheaper than a restaurant. There's a stand-up bar in the bakery across the street. (Behind the Madeleine Church, 26 Place de la Madeleine, metro: Madeleine, open 9:30-19:00, closed Sunday.) If you're hungry near Notre-Dame, the only grocery on the Ile de la Cité is tucked away in a small street running parallel to the church, one block north.

Here are a few restaurants I've enjoyed (listed by area):

Latin Quarter: **La Petite Bouclerie** (33 Rue de la Harpe, centre of touristy Latin Quarter) is a cosy place with good family cooking. £6.60 (66F) menu. **Restaurant Polidor** (41 Rue Monsieur-le-Prince, midway between Odéon and Luxembourg metro stops, tel. 43/26-95-34). Friendly Monsieur Millon runs this old turn-of-the-century-style place, great *cuisine bourgeoise*, vigorous local crowd, historic toilet, arrive by 19:00 to get a seat, meals £7-£10 (70-100F). **Atelier Maître Albert** (5 Rue Maître Albert, metro: Maubert-Mutualité, tel. 46/33-13-78) fills with Left Bank-types; best value is its nightly set dinner (serves dinner only, closed Sundays).

Rue Mouffetard, a street lined with colourful eateries, is a bit touristy, but has lots of choice and lots of fun food (metro: Monge). My favourites are **Le Clas Descartes** (8 Rue Descartes, tel. 43/25-44-94, £5.60 (56F) meals) and **Café Mouffetard** (116 Rue Mouffetard, closed Mondays).

Ile St. Louis: For crazy (but quite touristy) cellar atmosphere and hearty fun food, don't miss a feast at **La Taverne du Sergent Recruitier** (the 'Sergeant Recruiter' used to get young Parisians drunk and stuffed here, and then signed them into the army), centre of Ile St. Louis, three minutes from Notre-Dame, 41 Rue St. Louis, open Mon.-Sat. from 17:00, tel. 43/54-75-42; all you can eat for £13.80 (138F) including wine and service. There's a similar restaurant next door. **Aux Anysetiers du Roy** (61 Rue St. Louis en l'Ile, tel. 43/54-02-70, open 19:00-24:00, closed Wed. and August) serves another rowdy set meal with all the wine you want. You'll dine in tight quarters in a 400-year-old stone tavern for around £12 (120F).

Pompidou Centre: **Café de la Cité** (22 Rue Rambuteau, metro: Rambuteau, open daily except Sunday; inexpensive, popular, very French. £3.50 (35F) lunch specials. **Melodine** self-service right at the Rambuteau metro stop. For an elegant meal surrounded by lavish Art-Nouveau decor, dine at **Julien** (16 Rue du Faubourg

St. Denis, metro: Strasbourg-St. Denis, tel. 47/70-12-06; expect to spend £20 (200F).

Montmartre-Sacré Coeur: The *Butte* vibrates with colourful but touristy restaurants and crêperies at night. Just as colourful but tucked away from the commercial hubbub are **Butte en Vigne** (5 Rue Poulbot, towards the Eiffel Tower from Pl. du Tertre, vamp atmosphere, £7.70-£11 (77-110F) menus 46/06-91-96) and **Le Carillon de Montmartre** (18 Rue du Chevalier de la Barre, just behind the church to the right, tel. 42/55-17-26, good local food, reasonable price, closed Mondays and August).

Near Place de la Concorde: **André Faure** (40 Rue du Mont Thabor, metro: Concorde-Madeleine, tel. 42/60-74-28) serves basic hearty all-you-can-eat-and-drink French farm-style meals for a very good price. Mon.-Sat. 12:00-15:00, 19:00-22:30.

Near the Louvre: **L'Incroyable** (26 Rue de Richelieu, metro: Palais Royal, in a narrow passage between Rue de Montpensier 23 and Rue de Richelieu 26, open Tues.-Sat., 11:45-14:30, 18:30-20:30), serves (as the name hints) '*incroyable*' meals at an equally '*incroyable*' price—cheap.

Near Arc de Triomphe: **L'Etoile Verte** (the Green Star) at 13 Rue Brey, between Wagram and MacMahon, metro: Etoile, tel. 43/80-69-34, is a great working-class favourite, with £4.50 (45F) meals.

Near the recommended Hotel International: **Restaurant Chez Fernand** (17 Rue de la Fontaine au Roi, metro: Goncourt) is local and homely as they come, with good value and great Beaujolais.

Near Invalides and recommended hotels on Rue Cler: **Restaurant Chez Germaine** (30 Rue Pierre-Leroux, metro: Vaneau, tel. 42/73-28-34, open Mon.-Sat. 11:30-14:30, 18:30-21:00) is another small family place: go early to find a seat to eat well and cheap.

EUROPEAN FESTIVALS

Each country has a 'national day' celebration. A visit to a country during its national holiday can only make your stay more enjoyable. They are: Austria, October 26; France, July 14; Italy, June 2; Netherlands, April 30; Switzerland, August 1; West Germany, June 17.

Netherlands
Kaasmarkt: Fridays only from late April to late September, colourful cheese market with members of 350-year-old Cheese Carriers' Guild, Alkmaar, 15 miles north of Amsterdam.
North Sea Jazz Festival: weekend of third Sunday in July, world's greatest jazz weekend, 100 concerts with 500-plus musicians, The Hague.

Germany
Der Meistertrunk: Saturday before Whit Monday, music, dancing, beer, sausage in Rothenberg ob der Tauber.
Freiburger Weinfest: last Friday in June to following Tuesday, wine festival in Black Forest town of Freiburg.
Kinderzeche: weekend before third Monday in July to weekend after, festival honouring children who saved the town in 1640s, Dinkelsbuhl.
Trier Weinfest: Saturday to first Monday in August, Trier.
Gaubondenfest: second Friday in August for ten days, second only to Oktoberfest, Straubing, 25 miles southeast of Regensburg.
Der Rhein in Flammen: second Saturday in August, dancing, wine and beer festivals, bonfires, Koblenz to Braubach.
Moselfest: last weekend in August or first in September, Mosel wine festival in Winningen.
Backfischfest: last Saturday in August for 15 days, largest wine and folk festival on the Rhine, in Worms.
Wurstmarkt: second Saturday in September to following Tuesday, and third Friday to following Monday, world's largest wine festival, in Bad Durkheim, 25 miles west of Heidelberg.
Oktoberfest: starting third-to-last Saturday in September to first Sunday in October, world's most famous beer festival, Munich.

Austria
Salzburg Festival: July 26-August 30. Greatest music festival, focus on Mozart.

Italy
Sagra del Pesche: second Sunday in May, one of Italy's great

popular events, huge feast of freshly caught fish, fried in world's largest pans, Camogli, ten miles south of Genoa.
Festa de Ceri: May 15, one of the world's most famous folklore events, colourful pageant, giant feast afterwards, Gubbio, in hill country 25 miles northeast of Perugia.
Palio of the Archers: last Sunday in May, re-enactment of medieval crossbow contest with arms and costumes, Gubbio, 130 miles northeast of Rome.
Palio: July 2 and August 16, horse race is Italy's most spectacular folklore event, medieval procession beforehand, 35,000 spectators, Siena, 40 miles southwest of Florence.
Joust of the Saracen: first Sunday in September, costumed equestrian tournament dating from 13th century crusades against the Muslim Saracens, Arezzo, 40 miles southeast of Florence.
Historical Regatta: first Sunday in September, gala procession of decorated boats followed by double-oared gondola race, Venice.
Human Chess Game: first or second weekend in September in even-numbered years, medieval pageantry and splendour accompany re-enactment of human chess game in 1454, Basso Castle in Marostica, 40 miles northwest of Venice.

Switzerland

Landsgemeinde: first Sunday in May, largest open-air parliamentary session, Glarus, 40 miles southeast of Zürich.
Montreux International Jazz Festival: first to third weekends in July, comprehensive annual musical events featuring top artists, Montreux.
William Tell Plays: second Thursday in July to first Sunday in September, dramatic presentations retelling the story of William Tell, open-air theatre, Interlaken.
Swiss National Day: August 1, festive national holiday, parades, concerts, bell-ringing, fireworks, yodelling, boat rides, nationwide.

France

Fetes de la St. Jean: around June 24, three days of folklore and bulls running in streets, St. Jean de Luz, on the coast south of Bordeaux.
Tour de France: first three weeks of July, 2,000-mile cycle race around France ending in Paris.
Bastille Day: July 13 and 14, great national holiday all over France, Paris has biggest festivities.
Alsace Wine Fair: second and third weekends in August, Colmar.
Festival of Minstrels: first Sunday in September, wine, music, folklore, etc., Ribeauville, 35 miles south of Strasbourg.
Fete d'Humanité: second or third Saturday and Sunday in September, huge communist fair, colourful festivities—not all red, Paris.

EUROPE BY TRAIN

While this itinerary is designed for car travel, it can be adapted for train and bus. The trains cover all the cities very well but can be frustrating in several rural sections. This itinerary would make a three-week first class Eurailpass (£210 ($370), you must buy it outside Europe) worthwhile—especially for a single traveller.

Eurailers should know what extras are included on their pass— like any German buses marked "bahn" (run by the train company), boats on the Rhine, Mosel and Danube rivers and the Swiss lakes, and the Romantic Road bus tour.

A train/bus version of this trip requires some tailoring to avoid areas that are difficult without your own wheels and to take advantage of certain bonuses that train travel offers. Trains in this region are punctual and well-organised. Below is a plan which works well.

Day		Sleep in
1	Arrive in Haarlem	Haarlem
2	Haarlem, sightsee Amsterdam	Haarlem
3	Amsterdam—Arnhem—Koblenz— St. Goar	St. Goar
4	Cruise St. Goar—Bacharach	Bacharach
5	Train—Frankfurt, Romantic Road to Rothenburg	Rothenburg
6	Rothenburg, Romantic Road to Munich	Munich
7	Side-trip into Bavaria, castle	Munich
8	Munich	Night train
9	Venice	Venice
10	Venice—Florence	Florence
11	Florence—Orvieto—Bagnoregio/Civita	Bagnoregio
12	Bagnoregio—Orvieto—Rome	Rome
13	Rome	Rome
14	Rome	Night train
15	Cinque Terre beaches	Vernazza
16	More Italian Riviera	Night train
17	Bern and Alps	Gimmelwald
18	Hike in Alps	Gimmelwald
19	Interlaken—Bern—Basel—Colmar	Colmar
20	Colmar, Alsace Villages	Night train
21	Paris	Paris
22	Paris	Paris

YOUTH HOSTELS

Youth hosteling is the cheapest way to travel. Europe's 2,000 hostels, charging £2.50-£3.50 ($4-6) per night, provide kitchens for self-cooked meals. They have curfews (generally 23:00), mid-day lock-ups (usually 9:00-17:00), require sheets (you can rent one), membership cards and, except for southern Germany, are open to 'youths' from 8 to 80. (For a complete listing of Europe's 2,000 hostels, see the *International Youth Hostel Handbook*, Vol. 1.) Here are the hostels lying along our route:

Netherlands: *Amsterdam*—Stadsdoelen, Kloveniersburgwal 97, 1011 KB Amsterdam; 184 beds; Metro: Niewmarkt; bus 4, 5, 9, 16, 24, 25; tel. 020/246832. Vondelpark, Zandpad 5, Vondelpark, Vondelpark, 1054 GA Amsterdam; 300 beds; bus 1, 2, 3, 6, 7, 10; tel. 020/831744. *Haarlem*—Jan Gijzenpad 3, 2024 CL Haarlem-Noord; 108 beds; 3km bus 2, 6; tel. 023/373793.
Germany: *Bacharach*—Jugendburg Stahleck, 6533 Bacharach/Rhein; 207 beds; tel. 06743/1266; wonderful castle hostel, 15 minutes above town, view of Rhine. *Bingen-Bingerbruck*—Herter Str. 51, 6530 Bingen, Bingerbruck/Rhein; 194 beds; tel. 06721/32163. *Oberammergau*—Malensteinweg 10, 8103 Oberammergau; 130 beds; tel. 08822/4114. *Oberwesel*—Jugendgastehaus, Auf dem Schonberg, 6532 Oberwesel; 179 beds; tel. 06744/7046. *St. Goar*—Bismarckweg 17, 5401 St Goar; 150 beds; tel. 06741/388. *Rothenburg/Tauber*—Rossmuhle 8803 Rothenburg/Tauber; 141 beds; tel. 09861/4510. Spitalhof, Postfach 1206, 8803 Rothenburg/Tauber; 90 beds; tel. 09861/7889. *Creglingen*—Erdbacherstr. 30, 6993 Creglingen; 114 beds; tel. 07933/336.
Dinkelsbuhl—Koppengasse 10, 8804 Dinkelsbuhl; Open March 1-Oct 31; 510 beds; tel. 09851/509. *Munchen*—Wendl-Dietrich Str. 20, 8000 Munchen 19; tram 21, Rotkreuzplatz; 510 beds; tel. 089/131156. Jugendgastehaus, Miesingstr. 4, 8000 Munchen 70; tram 16, 26, Boschetsrieder Str.; 344 beds; tel. 089/7236550. *Pullach*—Munich, Burg Schwaneck, Burgweg 4-6, 8023 Pullach; 130 beds; tel. 089/7930643; a renovated castle. *Fussen*—Mariahilferstr. 5, 8958 Fussen; 150 beds; tel. 08362/7754.
Garmisch-Partenkirchen—Jochstr. 10, 8100 Garmisch-Partenkirchen; 290 beds; tel. 08821/2980.
Austria: *Reutte*—6600 Reutte, Prof. Dengel-Strasse 20, Tirol; 28 beds; tel. 05672/3039. *Reutte-Hofen*—6600 Reutte, Jugengastehaus am Graben, Postfach 3, Tirol; 38 beds; tel. 05672/264-4860. *Innsbruck*—6020 Innsbruck, Reichenauerstrasse 147, Tirol; 190 beds; tel. 05222/46179. Studentenheim, 6020 Innsbruck, Reichenauerstrasse 147; 112 beds; tel. 05222/46179. 6020 Inns-

bruck, Rennweg 17b, Tirol; 100 beds; tel. 05222/25814. 6020
Innsbruck, Sillg. 8a, Tirol; 100 beds; tel. 05222/31311. 6020
Innsbruck, Volkshaus, Radetzkystr. 47; 52 beds; tel. 05222/466682.
Italy: *Siena*—'Guido Riccio'. Via Fiorentina (Lo Stellino), 53100
Siena; 110 beds; tel. 0577/52212. *Venezia*—Fondamenta Zitelle 86,
Isola della Giudecca, 30123 Venezia; 320 beds; tel. 041/5238211.
Arezzo—Via Borg'Unto 6, 52100 Arezzo; 40 beds; tel. 0575/354546.
Cortona—Via Maffei 57, 52044 Cortona; 80 beds; tl. 0575/601765.
Firenze—Viale Augusto Righi 2-4, 50137 Firenze; 400 beds; tel.
055/601451. Ostello Santa Monaca, Via Santa Monaca 6, Firenze
26-83-38; unofficial, no card required. *Lucca*—'Il Serchio', Via
del Brennero (Salicchi), 55100 Lucca; 90 beds; tel. 0583/953686.
Roma—'Aldo Franco Pessina', Viale delle Olimpiadi 61 (Foro
Italico), 00194 Roma; 350 beds; tel. 06/3964709.
Switzerland: *Gimmelwald-Murren*—Beim Rest Schilthorn, 3826
Gimmelwald; 44 beds; tel. 036/55.17.04.
Grindelwald—Terrassenweg, 3818 Grindelwald; 133 beds; tel.
036/53.10.09. *Interlaken-Bonigen*—Aareweg 21, am See, 3806
Bonigen; 200 beds; tel. 036/22.43.53.
France: *Colmar*—7 Rue St Niklaas, 68000 Colmar (Haut-Rhin);
65 beds; tel. 89/41.33.08. *Paris*—8 Boulevard Jules Ferry,
75011 Paris; 99 beds; tel. 1/43-57-55-60. Choisy-le-Roi, 125 Avenue
de Villeneuve-St-Georges, 94600 Choisy-le-Roi; 280 beds; tel.
(16) 1/48-90-92-30. Auberge de Jeunesse Le D'Artagnan, 80 Rue
Vitrave, 75020 Paris, 400 beds, Mo: Porte de Bagnelet, tel.
1/43-61-08-75.